Move On

Move On

When Mercy Meets Your Mess

Vicki Courtney

W Publishing Group

An Imprint of Thomas Nelson

Published in Nashville, Tennessee, by W Publishing, an imprint of Thomas Nelson.

Thomas Nelson titles may be purchased in bulk for educational, business, fund-raising, or sales promotional use. For information, please e-mail SpecialMarkets@ThomasNelson.com.

Internet addresses, phone numbers, or company or product information printed in this book are offered as a resource and are not intended in any way to be or to imply an endorsement by Thomas Nelson, nor does Thomas Nelson vouch for the existence, content, or services of these sites, phone numbers, companies, or products beyond the life of this book.

Unless otherwise noted, Scripture quotations are taken from the Holy Bible, the English Standard Version. © 2001 by Crossway Bibles, a division of Good News Publishers.

Scripture quotations marked KJV are from the King James Version. Public domain.

Scripture quotations marked NASB are from the New American Standard Bible®, © The Lockman Foundation 1960, 1962, 1963, 1968, 1971, 1972, 1973, 1975, 1977, 1995. Used by permission.

Scripture quotations marked NIV are from the Holy Bible, New International Version®, NIV®. © 1973, 1978, 1984, 2011 by Biblica, Inc.™ Used by permission of Zondervan. All rights reserved worldwide.

Scripture quotations marked NLT are from *Holy Bible*, New Living Translation. © 1996, 2004, 2007. Used by permission of Tyndale House Publishers, Inc., Wheaton, Illinois 60189. All rights reserved.

Scripture quotations are also taken from *The Message* by Eugene H. Peterson. © 1993, 1994, 1995, 1996, 2000, 2001, 2002. Used by permission of NavPress Publishing Group.

Library of Congress Cataloguing-in-Publication Data

Courtney, Vicki.
  Move on : when mercy meets your mess / Vicki Courtney.
     pages cm
  Includes bibliographical references.
  ISBN 978-0-8499-6491-6 (trade paper)
  1. Integrity—Religious aspects—Christianity. 2. Honesty. 3. Grace (Theology) I. Title.
  BV4647.I55C68 2014
  248.4—dc23   2013051120

Printed in the United States of America

14 15 16 17 18 19 RRD 6 5 4 3 2 1

This book is dedicated in loving memory of my literary agent and dear friend, Lee Hough. He gave wings to my words and taught me that no matter how messy life gets, "God is good. God is faithful. God is merciful. God is loving."

Contents

The Mess That Changed Everything

On the morning of April 19, 2011, I pushed the Publish button on a blog post that changed the course of my ministry. Most important, it profoundly altered my view of God and allowed me to see His gift of grace and mercy in a new light. I opened the post with these words:

> Few would argue that the "Mom, I'm pregnant" announcement is at the top of a parent's list of knock-the-breath-out-of-you announcements you hope never to hear from your unmarried child. As someone who has written on the topic of sexual purity, I have stated often that my kids are not exempt when it comes to worldly temptations. I was humbly reminded of this fact a few weeks ago when my oldest son delivered the news, "Mom, I think Casey may be pregnant." Ryan and Casey are good kids who made a bad choice. Two months

into their engagement, they let their guard down, and as a result, they face a new challenge—shortly after marrying, they will become parents.

I want to give you a bit more background about that morning—just six weeks prior—when I learned about the pregnancy. Ryan had recently graduated from college and was living at home before the big wedding in July. His fiancée was finishing her last semester of college eight hundred miles away. When he left for work that morning, I was sitting in my living room in my favorite writing chair, reading over the final manuscript for a new Bible study for mothers of sons called *5 Conversations You Must Have with Your Son*. In my lap were the final page proofs for the book, and I was putting the finishing touches on Conversation #3: "Not everyone's doing it! (And other naked truths about sex you won't hear in the locker room)." Yep. It was all about sexual purity, and it provided some handy tips on how we as parents can encourage our sons to save sex for marriage. (In addition to the Bible study, I had also written a book by the same title, and it was due to hit the bookstore shelves just weeks after I made the announcement above on my blog. I'll go ahead and pause here and give you a minute to clear the lump in your throat regarding the irony of the rather awkward timing of my son's announcement.)

I was absorbed in proofing Conversation #3 when my boy walked back through the front door after leaving for work just fifteen minutes before. I assumed he had forgotten something, but when I saw the look on his face, I knew something wasn't right. It was one of those mother's-intuition moments. I immediately got up to meet him halfway as he made a beeline for me. He was ashen and his voice quaked. "Mom, I can't stand it any longer. I had to come back and tell you something."

My six-foot-one boy fell into my arms and mumbled through tears, "Mom, I think Casey may be pregnant." In that moment, I was not an author. I was not a speaker. There was no thought whatsoever of the parenting books I had written or the one that was about to release. In that moment, I was a mother and I did what any good mother would do. I cradled my boy in my arms, wept with him, and boldly reassured my son that, with God's help, we would get through this. I was a fellow sinner whose own life had been radically altered by the good news of God's amazing grace, and now it was my turn to administer that grace to my son. There was no pep talk. No "How could you?!" No condemnation. Only grace.

I shudder to think of what my response to my son might have been had I not already vowed to give up the pretender game a few years prior. You know the game—your life may be unraveling at the seams, but you paint on the trademark plastic smile and pretend like every day is rainbows and butterflies. And, in spite of my once-bold declaration to live in openness and transparency, I find that I still have a tendency to pull the game off the shelf from time to time, dust it off, and play another round. Old habits die hard. I like to think of myself as *real* and *authentic*, but until the day of my son's announcement, I had handpicked what I would allow to be exposed and what would remain covered. That buffet-style authenticity changed on that day.

When the blog post went live, comments began to pour in, and I held my breath. Like any mother who is bent on protecting her cubs, I was ready to do battle with anyone who dared to rob my children of the forgiveness and grace that was theirs to claim. I had been in ministry long enough to feel the sting of judgment that can come from my fellow brothers and sisters in Christ. And, dare I say, I've been that sister who at times has administered the same harsh sting of judgment. (More about that in a later chapter.) As I read through the comments that posted on that day, I was pleasantly surprised at the graciousness of God's people. There was no judgment, no suggested "Vicki Courtney Book Burning," no unsolicited advice about what might have been missing in my parenting arsenal of teaching—only grace. It was as if all of us—my family, my readers, and my audience—breathed a huge sigh of relief on that day as we came out of our hiding places to remind each other what God's grace really looks like.

As I read the comments from my fellow sisters and brothers, a passion to write this book was birthed in my heart. I realized that you, too, are exhausted from playing the pretender game, and many of you are desperate to remove your masks. You shared your own muddy messes and begged for the opportunity to be real and to emerge from the shame-laden trenches emboldened with a newfound brand of grace.

You wanted permission to be imperfect and to expose your own blemishes. Not permission to stay there, but permission to be a work in progress. And then it dawned on me. If more people could see this brand of Christianity, they would be beating down the doors of the church to get in. I honestly believe that. If we're looking for a successful evangelism strategy, this may be the one. Imagine a world where people are drawn to the life-changing displays of God's love in our own lives, rather than repelled by our harsh words of judgment and finger-pointing over the sins and imperfections of others.

I guess you could say that God staged an intervention in my life that day when my son dropped his bombshell news. A much-needed intervention. I've been in recovery in the days that have followed. And honestly, I hope I never recover from what He's taught me about His grace and mercy.

The truth is, we're all a mess. But the good news is that God is bigger than any of our muddy messes. Unfortunately, most Christians will live their entire lives attempting to clean up their messes on their own or, even worse, hide their messes under a multitude of modern-day fig leaves.

This book is for those of us who are weary of hiding and pretending. It's about finding the courage to come clean about the messes we are. To lay our hearts and souls bare before the Lord and say, "I'm not okay and I need Your help." But this book is also about finding the courage to come clean with each other and acknowledge our struggles and imperfections. To remove our masks and live wholehearted lives rather than the double-minded lives many of us have settled for. It's about saying good-bye to that person we've been pretending to be and celebrating the person God created: a gloriously imperfect mess who is loved by a perfect and holy God.

A Glorious, Beautiful Mess

This past weekend, I went on an evening boat ride with my family. We anchored the boat with the intent of doing some stargazing. My grandson is nearly two now, and to say he is obsessed with being in the water would be an understatement. One of his favorite things to do is jump off the deck of the boat and into someone's waiting arms. No sooner than we had put the anchor down, the chorus of pleas began. "Two-tree, two-tree, two-tree." That is his way of saying, "I want to do that thing where y'all count 'one, two, three,' and then I jump, okay?"

I watched as my daughter-in-law stripped him down to a diaper and life jacket. My son Ryan jumped into the water, and with his arms open, signaled for his boy to jump. Before Walker hit the water, he was already demanding "two-tree" again. Over and over again, he jumped. And over and over again, his daddy caught him. This went on for a dozen or more jumps; and then my son, growing tired, told his boy, no more. Time to get back on the boat and stay on the boat. Taking a cue that his daddy was officially off the clock, Walker immediately turned his attention to me and began saying, "Mimi, two-tree? Mimi, two-tree?" What began as a question quickly turned into a frantic and urgent request. "Mimi, two-tree! Mimi, two-tree!"

It was heart wrenching to see him screaming for another chance to jump into someone's arms. Look, I couldn't handle the peer pressure in my younger years, so what makes you think I stood a chance when my grandson was begging me with taunts of "Mimi, two-tree!"? So I did it. I jumped in. Fully clothed, I got up and took a running leap off the back of the boat. My reward was coming up for air and hearing the precious giggles of a two-year-old who didn't think there was anything unusual or odd about a fifty-year-old Mimi jumping into the lake with all her clothes on. I then assumed my rightful place in the water as my son lifted my grandson back up to the platform to begin his next round of jumps, this time into his Mimi's arms.

As I waited to catch my grandson for what seemed like the bazillionth time, I couldn't help but marvel in the reality of the moment. It hadn't been that long ago when I heard that announcement, "Mom, I think Casey might be pregnant." What a mess that was. And now, this: "Mimi, two-tree! Mimi, two-tree!" Mercy met us in our mess and turned it into something beautiful.

Coming clean about our struggles, weaknesses, and imperfections is a scary thing. It's a lot like jumping off the back of a boat and trusting that someone will catch you. Not only that, you want to know it will be worth it when you come up for air. From someone who's taken the jump, let me assure you, it's worth it. When you've experienced the mercy of God in the deep, staying on the boat and playing it safe is no longer an option.

So what do you say? Your Father is waiting with open arms.

"One . . . two . . . tree . . ."

Chapter 1

Cleanup on Aisle One!

*What would happen if one woman told the truth
about her life? The world would split open.*

—MURIEL RUKEYSER, "KÄTHE KOLLWITZ"

"Sometimes I feel like I'm playing a part I've been cast into, but it's not who I truly am." I fidgeted nervously in my seat as I shared this confession with a Christian counselor several years ago. My voice trailed off at the end and I quickly discounted the statement. "I'm sure it's just a phase I'm going through."

But he wouldn't let me evade the thought. "Let's stay there for a minute. Tell me more about what makes you feel that way."

I'd spent my entire life doing whatever it took *not* to "stay there." It had taken all the courage I could muster to walk into his office, much less make the confession. Now I wanted to retract my statement and go back to talking about things that were in my safe zone. Silence ensued. *Say something. Anything.* I attempted to deflect his statement with another excuse in a long line of excuses: "It's probably because my last child is about to leave the nest and I'm experiencing a bit of an identity crisis. No big deal." He nodded his head. More silence followed. *Dad-gummit, this guy is good.*

I glanced at the clock, desperate to make a getaway from the unfamiliar realm of "stay there." Thirty-five minutes left in the session. He smiled. "Go on."

I could either spill my guts or play an expensive round of the quiet game. I took a deep breath and continued, "Sometimes I feel like a fraud in ministry. It's not that I don't believe everything I teach and write about. I do. It's just that I'm reminded on a daily basis of how rarely I myself measure up to the truths I talk about." More silence followed. He knew I needed to say more, and he patiently waited. "I mean . . . I talk a lot about Jesus Christ being our 'everything,' but I spend my days trying to find satisfaction in a thousand different false gods. Honestly, I don't know why anyone buys my books. If they knew the real me and saw my long list of mess-ups, they'd ask for a refund. Especially if they followed my children around for long enough and realized they're far from perfect too." With every word I spoke, I felt a tiny surge of courage.

"And I'm so tired. I've been burned-out for nearly a decade, but I can't seem to slow down. I don't know how to be still. It seems like the more I do for the kingdom, the more distant

I feel in my relationship with the Lord." My eyes filled with tears as I followed with a burden I'd never spoken aloud before. "No matter how much I do, I never feel like I measure up. Not as a mother, a wife, a Christian. Behind the curtain of my life, I'm a mess."

When I left the counselor's office that day, I felt like a burden had been lifted. Breaking the silence felt good. Incredibly good. I had taken a necessary first step: admitting to the mess. My healing journey began when I finally granted myself permission *not* to be okay. Not to stay there forever, of course, but rather to acknowledge that *not being okay* is a perfectly normal part of the Christian journey. I walked into the counselor's office suffering from a spiritual midlife crisis. I was worn-out, confused, and just plain exhausted from years of trying to keep up the appearance of being a devoted follower. Add to that the pressure to manage the appearances of my children. My façade was beginning to crumble. And that was a very, very good thing. Had I not come to the powerful realization during this season of counseling that it's not only okay but perfectly normal to be a work in progress, I'm certain I would have plunged into full-out damage control when my son's unexpected pregnancy announcement came nearly two years later. Stepping into that counselor's office for the first appointment marked the beginning of the end of the pretender game in my life.

As I began to plumb the depths of my soul in the months that followed that initial counseling session, I realized that somewhere along the way, grace had shifted from being the solid foundation of my faith to becoming a mere footnote in my belief system. The transition was not a sudden event, but rather a process that snowballed slowly over many years. The love and compassion I once granted to unbelievers (or, for that matter, stumbling Christians) was gradually replaced with finger-pointing and judgment. Time spent reading God's Word began to feel like something I *had* to do rather than something I *wanted* to do. My heart-to-heart conversations with God became less frequent and more distant. Sharing the Good News with others became a chore on my spiritual to-do list rather than a privilege. Of course, falling short in these areas produced a never-ending cycle of guilt and condemnation that only left me feeling more distant from God. In desperation, I began to pray and ask God to "restore to me the joy of your salvation" (Ps. 51:12). Bottom line, I wanted my joy back. But first I had to determine where along the way my joy had taken a hike and, more important, why.

If my hunch is correct, many of you can relate. Maybe your once-vibrant faith has, over time, devolved into a familiar mediocrity. Perhaps you go through the motions like a well-rehearsed dance number, never stopping to consider if God even choreographed the routine. On the outside your faith is clean, polished, and most of all, predictable. But deep down in your soul, you wonder if your walk with God was supposed to be *more*. More adventurous. More exciting. More risky. Before you even allow your heart to believe such a thought, you squelch the nagging thought, knowing it would require change and, most likely, a departure from your standard comfort zone. So you go through the routine another day. You wake up the next day and start all over again. Days turn to months, months into years, and years lapse into decades. Chances are, you'll take that same routine to your grave. Unless something interrupts your tidy, well-groomed faith routine.

In the preface, I shared how God used my son and daughter-in-law's unexpected pregnancy as an opportunity to practice genuine authenticity in the midst of a mess.

Have you ever experienced a similar interruption? What was your mess?

A rebellious teenager?

A failed marriage?

An addiction? (And I'm not just talking about drugs.)

An unexpected diagnosis?

A stronghold of sin?

A mountain of debt?

A job loss?

A friend's deep betrayal?

An unfulfilled dream?

An empty nest?

An ongoing struggle with depression?

Life is messy. Many of us are left reeling from our messes, knocked off kilter when life takes a turn from the scripts we've plotted out for our lives. Why are we so caught off guard by the fact that life is chaotic and unpredictable? Why can't we accept that messes are inescapable in this life? We frantically rush to fix them, brush past them, or bury them deep. As a result, we deny the possibility that God intended the difficulties of life to become a small part of His bigger story. We cannot accept the idea that the heartbreaks and hurdles are meant to become trophies of His grace rather than secrets to be buried. The good news is this: Mercy is never far from us.

In her book *Becoming Myself*, author Stasi Eldredge says,

> You were born into a glorious mess, and we all have become something of a glorious mess ourselves. And in the midst of our mess, God has a thing for us. He does not despise our humanity or despair over our condition as we sometimes do. He does not turn his face away from us in our failings or our self-centeredness, as we would like to. He is not *surprised*. He is aware that we are but dust and our feet are made of clay, and he has made arrangements for us to not stay that way.[1]

God has made provision for us to move on beyond the things that often stall us in the journey of faith. However, many of us have mistakenly defined *moving on* as "burying, hiding, denying, ignoring, or running." Ironically, we can't move on until we meet God's mercy at the intersection of life's detours. How do you know if this has happened? You can't shut up about the encounter. It shifted your faith. It altered your view of grace. It caused you to view life through a different lens. Or perhaps the biggest telltale sign: you can't wait to point others to the same Mercy, whatever their mess.

I know the thought of taking a deeper look at your messes may sound daunting to some of you. Opening up those wounds goes against the grain of everything you've been conditioned (and even taught) to do. *Move on. Never look back. Get over it. Buck up, little camper.* Sure, those familiar clichés sound like good advice in theory, but do they really work in the long term? Nope. Most licensed professional counselors (the good ones) will tell you it's necessary to first take a deeper look at the things that have knocked you off course before you can deal with them and move on. Failing to do so keeps you imprisoned in the same old spiritual rut of pretending like everything is okay. You can be smiling on the outside and dying on the inside.

My prayer is that God would use this book as a tool to help us take a deeper look at our messes (both past and current) and rediscover His life-changing grace and mercy. Only then can we truly move on and, in turn, extend that same grace and mercy to others. The first step is giving ourselves permission not to be okay.

Admitting to the Mess

Back in the day, before DVDs and the ability to DVR shows or subscribe to them from Netflix, you had to plan your life around your favorite shows. This was especially true in the month of December, when you had one shot to watch animated Christmas classics, such as *Frosty the Snowman*, *A Charlie Brown Christmas*, and my personal favorite, *Rudolph the Red-Nosed Reindeer*. If ever there was a character that learned that it was okay not to be okay, it was Rudolph. Even though I knew the final outcome of the show, my heart ached every year during the scene in which he was teased by the other reindeer (and not allowed to play the reindeer games!). Clearly, the anti-bullying campaigns had yet to catch on at the North Pole.

Besides the appearance of the Abominable Snowman, which usually left me hiding behind the sofa, there was another scene in the show that left me feeling equally as uncomfortable. I always felt so sad during the scene with the poor, unclaimed misfit toys. An airplane that can't fly. A boat that sinks. A cowboy that rides an ostrich instead of a horse. A "Charlie" in the box rather than a "Jack" in the box. The water gun that shoots jelly instead of water. A train with square wheels. A bird that swims. These toys were deemed imperfect and therefore sentenced to live out the remainder of their lives sequestered on an island—The Island of Misfit Toys. Their plight is portrayed as a sad one, but perhaps the sadder story would be to know you are a misfit and live in an environment where you have to pretend you're not.

Does that resonate with you? I just described how it feels for some of us to walk into church each week. The very place where we should feel safe to peel back the veneer and expose the worst of messes has become the place of polite smiles and untruthful exchanges of, "I'm fine. How are you?" When we continue this charade, the truth about ourselves and the glorious truth about the gospel remain untold. No wonder the outside world wants nothing of this game.

The very essence of the gospel message tells us we're a

mess—each and every one of us. No one is exempt. Romans 3:23 reminds us, "For all have sinned and fall short of the glory of God" (NIV). We are all on equal turf when it comes to our contribution to the trashy landfill of sin. Some people's trash may smell worse than others, but at the end of the day, it all smells. Fortunately for us, God saw something worth redeeming out of our foul, rank trash heap.

In his book *The Ragamuffin Gospel*, Brennan Manning says, "For ragamuffins, God's name is Mercy. We see our darkness as a prized possession because it drives us into the heart of God. Without mercy our darkness would plunge us into despair—and for some, self-destruction. Time alone with God reveals the unfathomable depths of the poverty of our spirit."[2] It is in this very poverty of our spirits that we come to recognize we need a Savior. Yet few of us are willing to talk about the messy moments that lead us to the cross— or, for that matter, the messy moments that follow. Yes, we still find ourselves in the midst of messes after we are saved. We are *redeemed* creatures, not *perfect* creations. That won't happen this side of heaven.

One of my favorite passages of Scripture focuses on a Samaritan woman who encountered Jesus at a well. Jesus engaged her in a conversation about drawing water from the well in order that He might share about a different kind of water—living water.

Jesus said to her, "Everyone who drinks of this water will be thirsty again, but whoever drinks of the water that I will give him will never be thirsty again. The water that I will give him will become in him a spring of water welling up to eternal life." (John 4:13–14)

The woman is intrigued and responds, "Sir, give me this water." At this point, Jesus tells her to "Go, call your husband, and come here." When she replies that she has no husband, Jesus responds, "You are right in saying, 'I have no husband'; for you have had five husbands, and the one you now have is not your husband. What you have said is true" (vv. 15–18).

Jesus' statement begs the question: Why would Jesus tell her to go and call her husband if He already knew her story in advance? The answer: Jesus knew that living water was of no value to this woman unless she was first willing to acknowledge her mess. He called her out not to harass her or shame her, but rather to show her how desperately she needed what He was offering. Mercy met her in her mess, and the encounter forever changed her life. How do we know that? Because of how she responds after her encounter with the Messiah.

We know she didn't bury her shame or return to her old way of life because John 4:28–29 tells us, "The woman left her water jar and went away into town and said to the people, 'Come, see a man who told me all that I ever did. Can this be the Christ?'" The same woman who went to gather water in the middle of the day to avoid the judgmental whispers and scowls of disapproval from others runs to tell others about her unexpected collision with Mercy.

A true encounter with God's mercy will do that to you. It takes you from the depths of despair and leaves you wanting to shout from the rooftops. With shame and despair lifted away by nail-scarred hands of love, we can freely (and gladly!) tell others where to meet Mercy.

Here's where the story gets really exciting, but most people speed past it: "Many Samaritans from that town believed in him because of the woman's testimony, 'He told me all that I ever did'" (v. 39). Read that verse again. I'm struck by the phrase "because of the woman's testimony." Many believed in Jesus because she was willing to talk about her mess and, more important, her encounter with the Messiah. What if she had been silent after the encounter, burdened by shame? What if she had kept quiet, afraid of what others would think of her? Isn't that what many of us have done with our messes? Not just in regard to our past sins, but also with our current flaws, weaknesses, and imperfections? What if we defied conventional church culture and said, "Yep! I'm a ragamuffin. I am a heaping mess, but I am deeply loved by my Savior." I can think of no greater legacy than to have it said about me, "Many believed in Him because of Vicki Courtney's testimony of how Mercy met her in her mess." What about you?

Messy People Welcome Here

When we can freely admit to the messes we are, we can extend grace to others. Rather than pointing to the weaknesses and shortcomings of others and wondering why they can't get it together and be more like us (the pretend, fake versions of us), we are reminded of the current messes we are and the messes we've been in the past. Here's the crazy irony—others are already like us, not because they are perfect but because they are messes too! We're all in this together. All believers—from Billy Graham to the crackhead who just found Jesus—are equal at the foot of the cross. Yet few of us feel that camaraderie when we walk into church on Sunday morning.

It brings to mind a song by Casting Crowns called "Stained Glass Masquerade" that asks the question, "Are we happy plastic people?"[3] Imagine the feeling of freedom and acceptance of belonging to a church where imperfect people are welcome to come and admit that they are indeed imperfect. Studies indicate that church attendance is on the decline, and I can't help but wonder if part of the downward slide can be attributed to the fact that many of our churches have ceased to be hospitals for messed-up people and opted instead to become showrooms for polished pretenders.

I am grateful to be a part of a church that doesn't subscribe to the "stained glass masquerade." We are able to breathe a sigh of relief when we walk through the doors on Sunday mornings and be our imperfect selves. One of our pastors has shared openly from the pulpit about his ongoing struggle with depression. My husband and I teach a Sunday-morning Bible study class to young couples and share openly about past struggles in our marriage, along with other difficulties we experience on a day-to-day basis. I recently shared with the class about my own personal struggle with lapsing into legalistic thinking (more about this in a future chapter). My husband has shared with the class about a struggle with crippling anxiety he wrestled through in his thirties. As we have opened up, our class members have felt free to do the same. One member shared about his struggle with anger. Another member shared about her tendency to be materialistic. From my experience in my church, I can tell you that it is life-giving and hope-infusing to be a part of a community where it is safe to be your messy self rather than a polished pretender.

If your current church is not a safe haven for messy people, maybe God is calling you to be a catalyst for change. One of my passions in writing this book is to put God's grace back in the spotlight where it belongs. When we share our own personal testimonies about our life-changing encounters with God, it is contagious. It attracts rather than repels. Show me a church composed of real people who aren't afraid to acknowledge and talk about their flaws, and chances are, it's a growing church. If, on the other hand, vulnerability is met with the cold legalism of others, then prayerfully consider finding a place where authenticity is the focal point.

Get Real

I've always been bothered by the familiar phrase, "Stay true to yourself," or some version thereof. Even Shakespeare endorsed this mind-set in his oft-repeated quotation, "This above all: to thine own self be true."[4] I suppose the phrase bothers me because I'm a writer, and by default I overanalyze the meaning of words. I tend to think words mean something. That said, I don't want to stay true to myself—at least the part of myself that's prone to sin. I have lived long enough in this world to know what I'm capable of—and I'm fairly certain I would be a total disaster if I stayed true to my every desire, thought, and whim. Would we tell a friend who is having an affair to stay true to her impulses or feelings? Would we advise someone struggling with a same-sex attraction to stay true to her urges? Would we tell someone who is dangerously overweight to stay true to her addiction to food? Or someone with a drinking problem to have one more drink if that's her heart's desire in that moment? That is pop psychology, current-culture, "if it feels good, do it" nonsense. Most of us have learned the hard way that staying true to our base desires can produce devastating consequences if we are allowed to define for ourselves what is "true."

Search the Bible over, and you'll find nothing that speaks to this idea of *finding ourselves* or *staying true to ourselves*. However, Scripture speaks volumes about our need to be true to God and His purposes in creating us. It speaks to the idea of finding our identity in Christ rather than in our desires, passions, and pursuits, in our own sinful humanity. It speaks about finding our purpose in life by submitting to God's will and direction, not our own faulty true north. It speaks of discovering our spiritual gifts and using them to point to the goodness and glory of God, not pointing to us.

Our goal is not to stay true to ourselves, but rather to stay true to the person God created us to be. However, we cannot discover the person God created us to be without first taking an honest look at our lives. Being honest with others and ourselves about our messes requires laying our hearts and souls bare before a loving God on a consistent basis. In 2 Corinthians 13:5, Paul challenged believers: "Examine yourselves, to see whether you are in the faith. Test yourselves." *The Message* says it this way: "Test yourselves to make sure you are solid in the faith. Don't drift along taking everything for granted. Give yourselves regular checkups." When my youngest son played high school football, he was required to undergo a heart screen at the beginning of the season as a preventative measure. If there had been a cause for concern, the screen would have likely tipped us off before he headed onto the field on game day.

In a similar fashion we as believers are called to examine our hearts on a consistent basis to uncover the issues that we so easily sweep under the rug in an effort to look okay on the outside. In Psalm 26:2, we are called to test our hearts and our minds. The New Living Translation says, "Put me on trial, LORD, and cross-examine me. Test my motives and my heart." When I read that statement, I picture being in a courtroom where a defendant is being cross-examined by an attorney who has made it his mission to uncover the truth. That picture is intimidating to say the least. But Christ does not play the part of the prosecuting attorney. He is our Defender. First John 2:1 describes Christ as "an advocate with the Father" when we sin. He's on our side, our Defender, our Mediator who intercedes for us (Heb. 7:25). Psalm 26:3 reminds us, "For your steadfast love is before my eyes." That steadfast love heals us. That unending, always-sticks-by-us love enables us to come out of our caves of shame and into the light of His mercy.

Most of us are hesitant to examine our hearts for fear of what we might find there. We have nothing to fear when we keep the steadfast love of the Lord as our faithful guide. His unfailing love gives us the courage to admit our struggles, open our wounds, expose our shame, and confess our sin. Living an authentic, vibrant, *real* faith requires us to admit we are under construction but deeply loved by God in the restoration process.

You might remember the classic tale *The Velveteen Rabbit*, in which a toy rabbit discovers what it means to become real.

"Does it hurt?" asked the Rabbit.

"Sometimes," said the Skin Horse, for he was always truthful. "When you are Real you don't mind being hurt."

"Does it happen all at once, like being wound up," he asked, "or bit by bit?"

"It doesn't happen all at once," said the Skin Horse. "You become. It takes a long time. That's why it doesn't happen often to people who break easily, or have sharp edges, or who have to be carefully kept. Generally, by the time you are Real, most of your hair has been loved off, and your eyes drop out and you get loose in the joints and very shabby. But these

things don't matter at all, because once you are Real you can't
be ugly, except to people who don't understand."[5]

"It doesn't happen all at once. . . . *You become*."

When you choose to be real, you embark on a journey.
It is not a journey for the fragile or faint of heart. Showing
up at the starting line will require courage. It's far easier to
blend into the crowd and pretend all is well and good. Smile,
learn your lines, and join the ranks of the status quo. If you
want to be real, you must be willing to put up a fight. Others
will be uncomfortable with your honesty. Many will label
you as odd or emotional or even unspiritual. You will meet
resistance at every turn. You will stand alone (or with some
fellow ragamuffins) against the norm, because real people
are not content to sit on the sidelines and remain silent about
the power of the gospel. You'll know they are real when you
can't help but get a glimpse of Jesus when you are in their
presence.

I'm not referring to a spill-your-guts, no-healthy-
boundaries, TMI kind of real where you vent about your
marriage struggles on Facebook or hash out the details of
your past during an open mic session at church. I'm talking
about the kind of real where you offer glimpses of your story
in order to put a spotlight on grace. Interestingly, the Greek
word for *grace* is *charis*, which means "the divine influence
upon the heart and its reflection in the life."[6] Is your life a
reflection of God's grace?

Psalm 51:6 is an anthem for authenticity: "Behold, you

delight in truth in the inward being, and you teach me wisdom in the secret heart." *The Message* says it this way: "What you're after is truth from the inside out. Enter me, then; conceive a new, true life." I love that. *A new, true life.* No more pretending. No more saying we're okay when we're really not. No more pressure to keep it all together and keep it all hidden. It's about giving ourselves permission to be honest about the *whole* journey of faith, our muddy messes included, not just the highlight reel we broadcast to others. The choice is simple: you can stay where you are—or you can get real and move on.

COMING CLEAN

As we journey together through this book, my hope is that you will pause to respond to how God is speaking to your heart in this process, so each chapter will conclude with some questions intended for encouragement and reflection. I hope that they encourage and challenge you as we seek to know God's heart for us more and more throughout this journey.

1. Could you relate to my confession in the counselor's office that "sometimes I feel like I'm playing a part I've been cast into, but it's not who I truly am"?
2. What messes has God used to "stage a much-needed intervention" to force you to reexamine your faith?

3. Reflect on this statement: "I know the thought of taking a deeper look at your messes may sound daunting to some of you. Opening up those wounds goes against the grain of everything you've been conditioned (and even taught) to do. *Move on. Never look back. Get over it. Buck up, little camper.*" Does the idea of looking at your messes bring you anxiety or relief? Or a bit of both?

4. How would you characterize your church? Is it a hospital for broken people or a showroom for polished pretenders?

5. Is it difficult for you to be real about your difficulties and imperfections? If so, ask God for courage. He offers it in abundant supply.

Chapter 2

Sanitized for Your Protection

*The Lord's mercy often rides to the door of our
heart upon the black horse of affliction.*

—Charles H. Spurgeon

I can still remember the first official women's event I ever attended. I had been a believer for a few short years, and prior to the event, I had only attended a handful of Christian retreats for college students. Women's events were not a common occurrence back in the late 1980s, so it was a rare treat to worship together with women from other churches and to hear a keynote speaker. I was excited because I was attending with a small group of women from my church, and we had booked several hotel rooms to stay overnight. And as a new mom I looked forward to getting a twenty-four-hour break from my mom duties.

I wasn't sure what to expect as our group settled into our seats with our Bibles and notebooks in our laps. I don't recall many details about the event, but I remember singing "Amazing Grace" just before the main speaker stepped up on the stage. It was a sweet time of worship, especially at the end when the male vocalist signaled the pianist to stop playing on the final chorus as a harmony of sweet voices rose to the heavens.

> *Amazing Grace, how sweet the sound,*
> *That saved a wretch like me.*
> *I once was lost but now am found,*
> *Was blind, but now I see.*[1]

It hadn't been that long since I had collided with this grace we were singing about, and my life had been forever changed. Unlike my Christian sisters in our group who grew up teething on the church pews and sharing testimonies of praying to receive Christ at Vacation Bible School or summer youth camp, my conversion played out like the chorus: "That saved a wretch like me. I once was lost but now am found, was blind, but now I see." I wiped away a few tears as I experienced flashbacks of my prior life while singing the words to the classic hymn. It was a powerful moment as the song ended and a silence fell upon the room.

The worship leader said a prayer and then welcomed the speaker up onto the stage. She looked every bit the part of what I'd imagined a Christian speaker to look like. Graceful and polished. Together. Refined. She was dressed in her Bible Belt–approved, Sunday-morning finery, right on down to her nylon panty hose. Her hair helmet was held firmly in place, tamed and shellacked with a heavy glaze of Aqua Net. She greeted us with a warm Southern drawl and then opened her message by reading a poem her husband had written and snuck into her suitcase just before she left. I don't remember any of the lines in the poem, but I do remember that it offered the first of many glimpses into her seemingly perfect life. By the end of the day, we would walk away wishing we had her perfect husband, her perfect marriage, her perfect children, and most of all, her perfect faith. Sigh.

As I listened to her, I longed to hear just *one* thing about her life that wasn't perfect. Anything. Was life ever hard for her? Did she and her husband ever fight? Did her children ever talk back? Did she ever get angry when people cut her off on the freeway? Did she struggle with gossip or overspending? Had she ever suffered a heartache that left her confused and questioning the presence of God? What was her amazing grace story? Had she ever felt like the "wretch" we had just sung about?

While I learned some new truths and scribbled them down on the blank pages of my notebook, I didn't feel like I could relate to her as a person. In fact, I walked away wondering if I was the only one in the room who still struggled in the aftermath of my amazing grace encounter.

Most of us are familiar with the quip, "If it sounds too good to be true, it probably is." Such was the case with our speaker. A couple of years later, I heard she and her perfect, poem-writing husband had divorced. If trouble was brewing in paradise when she spoke at the event I attended, she sure did a fantastic job of hiding it. I'm certainly not suggesting that she owed it to the audience to share about her marriage problems in vivid detail. However, she would have gained respect and credibility if she had been willing to acknowledge even a teeny-tiny chink in her armor. After I heard about her struggles, I couldn't help but wonder how long she had played the pretender game before her carefully constructed tower of cards began to tumble. Sadly, like so many others in the Christian spotlight who take a tumble, she silently disappeared from the ministry landscape altogether. And I learned a valuable lesson: you don't always know what's going on behind the curtain of someone's life.

I'm *Not* Great, How Are You?

When it comes to playing the pretender game, I certainly have no room to judge. I played quite a few rounds in my early years as a new believer. *Grin and bear it, but for heaven's sake, don't share it.* We've all been there. "Hey, how are you?" "I'm great! And you?" No one really expects an honest answer to that question unless you're paying a hundred dollars an hour for a scheduled counseling session. During lunch recently, I asked the same question to a friend I hadn't seen in a while and was caught off guard when she gave me an honest answer in return. I was grateful, but nonetheless a bit surprised.

My friend opened up about her painful struggle with infertility and the years of heartbreak when she didn't conceive. She shared about the litany of tests and never-ending doctors' appointments in her desperate search for answers and solutions. She shared about the tortuous roller-coaster cycle of getting her hopes up about a promising option only to have them dashed when it didn't result in pregnancy. Over and over again, hope inflated and hope destroyed. She explained that she and her husband were planning to try one last option. Her words were laced with a purposeful hesitancy. I reached across the table and grabbed her hand as I expressed my heartfelt sorrow over her infertility struggle. I asked one more question, and I knew the answer before I even formed the words, but I asked it anyway: "Lindsey, how's your faith doing?" She pursed her lips and replied with a raw honesty, "I won't lie to you. I'm angry at God. Very angry. I don't understand why He's allowing this."

I appreciated her honesty. I didn't have any quick-fix answers for her other than to reassure her that God "is near to the brokenhearted" (Ps. 34:18). The last thing Lindsey needed from me was a pep talk about how God expects her to scream, "Hallelujah, thank You, and amen!" every time she sees another negative reading on a pregnancy test. She might have felt distant in her relationship with the Lord in the midst of the dark pit she was in, but He was still there. He was lovingly pursuing her in the valley of her suffering whether she felt God's presence or not. Psalm 147:3 reminds us that "He heals the brokenhearted and binds up their wounds."

The enemy would love nothing more than for us to feel isolated and alone in our struggles, and he would be thrilled for us to abandon our faith when what we believe about Jesus doesn't match the circumstances we find ourselves in. However, when we take off our masks and share openly about our burdens, we invite others to share in our suffering process, and the Spirit knits our hearts together so that we don't feel quite so alone. Many Christians are reluctant to talk about what they are *really* thinking and feeling because, like Lindsey, they may be entertaining doubts about God. Many have concluded that if they aren't experiencing the pre-prescribed Christian response of peace (or the super-spiritual response of joy) in the wake of affliction, they should keep their reality to themselves. They certainly don't want to risk judgment or, even worse, chastisement for being weak in faith. Sadly, this is a justified concern in response to the disappointing glances and holier-than-thou comments of fellow believers. I wonder how many Christians have taken a permanent leave of absence from their faith because their churches and Christian circles of friends did not offer a safe place to process their doubts about God in the midst of adversity.

God's Purpose in Hardship

Like Lindsey, many of us are caught off guard when we encounter trials, and as a result, our faith takes a beating. It's normal to question why God acts in some situations and yet remains silent in others. This past month, one friend had to commit her teenage son to a residential treatment facility for dangerous behaviors, another friend lost a family member to a drug overdose, another friend was experiencing chronic pain, and a pastor's wife contacted me to share that her teenage son and his teenage girlfriend just announced they are expecting a baby.

All of these women faced the same choice when hurled unwillingly into their darkest moments: they could run headlong into Mercy's arms in the midst of their mess, link arms with the Great Comforter, and ride out the storm side by side, or they could turn their backs on God in defiance and go it alone. I'm happy to say each of my friends found shelter from her storm in the safe and strong arms of God.

Why do some people turn to God in the face of adversity, while others turn away from Him? Every person's story is different, but it's safe to say those who turn to Him have come to understand two basic truths about God: (1) His plans and purposes are higher than our capacity to understand them, and (2) He never promised His children a life free from struggles. In other words, no one is exempt from adversity. Unless those two foundational beliefs constitute the core of a believer's faith, it will be very difficult to surrender to God's purpose when experiencing times of hardship. Whether our hardship falls into the category of a temporary struggle or an ongoing thorn in the flesh, or whether we are holding in our hearts the pieces of a broken dream, a painful rejection, or a devastating tragedy, God stands ready to meet us in our mess and to reassure us that nothing is wasted in His economy. Every struggle has purpose.

Romans 5:3–5 reminds us: "Not only that, but we rejoice in our sufferings, knowing that suffering produces endurance, and endurance produces character, and character produces hope, and hope does not put us to shame, because God's love has been poured into our hearts through the Holy Spirit who has been given to us." The Greek word for *produces* is *katĕrgazŏmai* (kat-er-gad´-zom-ahee), which means "to accomplish, finish, or fashion."[2] The word refers to a *process* that occurs over time rather than a one-time *event*. God is refining our faith, much like the smelting process that takes place with silver, gold, and other precious metals.

Isaiah 48:10 says, "Behold, I have refined you, but not as silver; I have tried you in the furnace of affliction." God uses the struggles and afflictions in our lives to mold us into the likeness of His Son. Rarely do we recognize this refining process when we are in the dark valley of despair. In His mercy, He picks up the broken pieces of our lives, not allowing a single scrap to go to waste, and uses them to cast us into a new creation.

When I reflect on the refining process, I think of the miracle of the butterfly. When we see the beauty of a butterfly as it takes flight, we often forget that this gorgeous creation once began as an ugly larva. Once the larva is contained in its cocoon, it is completely transformed before it emerges as a beautiful butterfly. Yet in order to emerge from that cocoon, it must be willing to put up a fight as it struggles to free itself from the cocoon. If this process of breaking out of the cocoon is somehow shortened and the butterfly is released prematurely, it will never be able to fly because its wings have not had sufficient time and resistance to develop its tiny muscles.

When his brothers threw him into a pit and sold him into slavery at the young age of seventeen, I doubt Joseph recognized a purpose in his suffering as he sat in that dirty abyss. He probably didn't recognize God's hand during the eleven years he spent in Potiphar's house or in the two years he spent in prison after being unfairly accused by Potiphar's wife of a crime he did not commit. Yet God was hard at work behind the scenes of his life to fulfill and reveal the purpose of his suffering. Only after Joseph was released from prison and his struggle was complete did he begin to see God's purpose in his many years of hardship. When he came face to face with his brothers twenty-two years after they had thrown him into the pit, he boldly declared,

> "I am your brother, Joseph, whom you sold into Egypt. And now do not be distressed or angry with yourselves because you sold me here, for God sent me before you to preserve life. . . . So it was not you who sent me here, but God. He has made me a father to Pharaoh, and lord of all his house and ruler over all the land of Egypt." (Gen. 45:4–5, 8)

I wonder how many of us would have given up on God the minute we landed in the bottom of the pit. I wonder how many of us are still sitting in our own modern-day pits, stewing about our circumstances and blaming God for the untimely relocation.

My friend, He never intends for you stay there forever. And He *never* wants you to conclude you are alone. Mercy waits for you in the pit. Do you see Him there? Look past the fog of your emotions and questions and doubts to see Him. Take hold of His hand and let Him help you out. I can't promise you an easy road, nor can I promise that the journey out of the pit is an overnight trip, but I can assure you of this: God will never leave your side. He will never forsake you. He will walk this journey with you, every step of the way, and He will fulfill His purpose in the midst of your pain. Only with Mercy by your side can you move on and make peace with your season of suffering.

Giving Thanks in the Desert Place

Most of us have heard the challenge in James 1:2 to "Count it all joy . . . when you meet trials of various kinds." And if you're like me, you probably grumbled under your breath, "Yeah, right." Few turn cartwheels and shout, "Hurray!" when we face an unexpected encounter with adversity. Let's be honest. It's hard enough to "count it all joy" when the trials are of the ordinary sort—a sick child, a breakup, a job loss, marriage struggles, a house that won't sell. But is *joy* even a word you can say out loud when you are experiencing the brand of adversity that transports you straight to the desert place? When I say "desert place," I am referring to the knock-the-breath-out-of-you moments when you wonder if you will be able to breathe again, much less smile or laugh. Your marriage ends. Your husband dies. A crippling injury. A terminal illness. A prodigal child. You know, the *doozies*. *Joy* is not the first word that comes to mind in the desert place. *Survival* maybe, but not *joy*.

I was so intrigued by the word *joy* in James 1:2 that I looked up the original Greek word to try to grapple with understanding how God could ask that of us. The Greek word for *joy* is *chara* (khar-ah´), which means "cheerfulness or calm delight."³ This type of joy is not a sudden burst of euphoria. This kind of joy doesn't get your heart pumping or leave you smiling uncontrollably from ear to ear. It is an established pattern or a way of life. It is a learned process. *A calm delight* is not manufactured in a moment. It is practiced over the course of many moments, hours, days, and months.

Notice also that joy is not linked to the actual occurrence. James didn't tell believers, "Count it all joy that your spouse just broke your heart," or "Be joyful that your child is facing cancer." It says count it joy "because you know that the testing of your faith produces perseverance. Let perseverance finish its work so that you may be mature and complete, not lacking anything" (James 1:3–4 NIV). Joy is not linked to the circumstances. It is linked to the *end result* of the circumstances. Joy comes because there is purpose, meaning, and a finished work. Our joy is connected to God's handiwork and presence in the midst of the desert.

We'd be masochists to be joyful in the very moment our hearts are breaking.

When I think of this kind of *chara* or joy, I think of the worship song "Blessed Be Your Name." The song is a beautiful example of experiencing a calm delight in the desert place. If we're honest, it's a lot easier to say "Blessed be Your name" when the streams of abundance flow. The desert place? Not so much. Oh sure, I can raise my hands in praise when I'm on the other side of the desert place because I've witnessed His faithfulness, but it becomes a bit harder when the desert place is my current zip code. Committing to say "Blessed be Your name" when we're smack-dab in the middle of the desert place is like agreeing to a part in a play before seeing the script.

I found myself in the desert place several years ago when I suffered a rejection and betrayal that was so painful I had to see a counselor to help me sort through the mess. It involved someone very close to me, so the wound was all the deeper. I was able to mumble out a "Blessed be Your name," sandwiched in between "Why me, God?" and "Please, please, heal my broken heart." He heard my cries. He understood my feelings of rejection. He met me in that desert place, plopped down next to me, and whispered His truths back into my heart while I sifted sand through my fingertips. I felt His clear presence through the trial and understand now how it's possible to experience a calm delight in the middle of the storm.

We all will experience the desert place at some point in

our lives. My literary agent found himself in the desert place when a string of headaches led to an MRI scan that revealed a malignant brain tumor. He had a headache one day and a death sentence the next. Another friend of mine was suddenly launched into the desert place when she received a phone call from her husband when he was out of town on business. He told her he had been arrested for soliciting a prostitute and would need her to bail him out. They were both Sunday school teachers at their local church. My friend's world was turned upside down with a single phone call. Another friend is currently living in the desert place because her wayward teen has run away countless times and recently threatened to take his life.

The desert place most feared by every parent is—without question—the loss of a child. One of our dearest couple friends, Barbara and Damon, were relocated to the desert place suddenly and without warning in October of 2006 when they lost their beautiful (and only) daughter, Lauren, at the age of twenty-one. Married for about a year, Lauren's husband had served in Iraq. He was home on furlough, but no one recognized the signs of post-traumatic stress disorder (PTSD) he was experiencing. One evening, just weeks before he was due to deploy to Iraq for a longer tour of duty, he shot Lauren while she slept and then turned the gun on himself. No one saw it coming.

When Lauren failed to show up for work the next day and her parents were unable to reach her, Damon went by their house to check on them and collided with the unspeakable tragedy. My husband and I were among a handful of people called to Barbara and Damon's home shortly after Damon returned home and broke the news to Barbara. To this day I remember sitting in their living room with my husband and our other dear friends, Donnie and Carolyn. We wept with Barbara and Damon. We prayed with them. At one point Barbara got up, walked into her bedroom, and crawled into her bed. Carolyn and I followed after her and crawled right into the bed with her. We wept some more. We prayed some more. We begged God to show our friends the way out of the desert place. In the meantime we made sure they knew they weren't there alone.

After taking several weeks off, Damon and Barbara returned one Sunday to church, where he is the worship minister and Barbara sings on the praise team. And just like so many Sundays before, Damon stepped up on the platform and began to lead worship as Barbara joined him onstage as part of the praise team. Do you know what they sang? "Blessed Be Your Name"! Through tears they continued singing: *On the road marked with suffering.*[4] And then I could hardly believe my eyes. They raised their hands in praise and lifted their eyes heavenward. And they continued singing. There was not a dry eye in the place that morning.

Could you sing those words if you were in my friends' shoes? Of course, their pain and heartache didn't magically disappear in that moment. Their hearts still ache over the loss of their only daughter. That ache will never go away. In the years to follow, they will find themselves retreating back to the desert place, and when they do, they will again face a choice: focus on their sorrow or focus on their Savior.

Life is uncertain. As my friends discovered, the forecast can change at any time. If you've set the sails of your faith to a forecast of sunny days, don't be surprised if it runs aground when the winds kick up and the storm clouds come rolling in. Charles Spurgeon once said, "Whether our days trip along like the angels mounting on Jacob's ladder to heaven or grind along like the wagons that Joseph sent for Jacob, they are in each case ordered by God's mercy."[5] He gives and takes away. What will your heart choose to say right now, in this moment, before the storm clouds gather? When we commit in advance to count it all joy or rejoice in various trials, that doesn't mean our emotions will match our declaration at the moment of impact. It simply acknowledges a vote of confidence in God's presence and His ability to bring good from whatever struggle, heartache, or dark valley may intersect our lives in the future. It is a *chara* kind of joy—a calm trust that Mercy will be by our side in the desert place, grieving right along with us.

Mercy Gives Back

While watching the national news one evening, I was moved to tears over a story about a camp that reunites foster children with their siblings who have been placed in separate homes. For some of the siblings it is the first chance to spend time with their brothers and sisters. In addition to providing standard camp activities and games, the camp also provides a time during which the siblings can come together and celebrate one another's birthdays since they have missed being together over the past years. The kids can pick out a gift (among donated items) for their sibling, wrap the gift, help decorate a cake, and then come together to swap gifts and sing a round of "Happy Birthday." Watching the footage of the kids blowing out their candles and hugging their siblings was almost more than I could bear.

The visionary behind the camp is a woman who had spent many years in the foster care system herself. When she was eight years old, she discovered she had a biological sister who had been placed in a different home. The two were not given an opportunity to spend time with each other until they were out of the foster care system in their young adult years. Now camps are held across the country to offer foster children what the two sisters had missed: an opportunity to get to know and bond with each other when they were younger. They decided to turn their own personal loss into a gain for others.

Mercy doesn't just show up in our mess and minister to our need of the moment. He promises to take our hand and move us beyond the mess and to use that mess to help others out of the desert place. If we fail to see God's purpose in our struggles, hardships, and devastating heartbreaks, we underestimate our encounter with His mercy. God uses our struggles and hardships to mold and prepare us for a higher purpose—a destiny, if you will. Our journey out of the desert doesn't end at the oasis. He wants to move us beyond that into caring for others out of our own experiences. What is your struggle? Whether it is a temporary situation, an ongoing thorn in the flesh (2 Cor. 12:7–10), or a season of suffering, God wants to use it as part of His bigger story.

You Are Not Alone

When we open up to others about our struggles, others can walk with us in the valley. We don't have to walk alone. Remember my sweet friend Lindsey who was struggling with infertility and wondering where God was in the midst of her heartache? She eventually decided to start a blog and chronicle her infertility journey. She brought her struggle out of the darkness and exposed it to the light. In doing so, she invited others to come alongside her as she walked her difficult road. This is what it looks like to live out Galatians 6:2, where Paul told us to "bear one another's burdens." God calls us to share our burdens, not bear them alone. As a beautiful footnote to Lindsey's story, she recently announced that she is expecting a baby and is documenting her pregnancy on her blog. Mercy met Lindsey in her mess. Regardless of whether or not she ever held a child of her own, God's divine plan was to bring beauty from the ashes.

Maybe you aren't experiencing a struggle right now and think you're off the hook when it comes to sharing your burdens. Not so fast! Let me ask you this: Do you make it a practice to talk about your past struggles, and more important, your encounters with God's mercy? When we refuse to talk about our past struggles and the messy moments of life, we fail to tell the whole story of our lives. We miss God-ordained moments to receive the "God of all comfort" from others in the midst of our struggles, and we miss the opportunity to give the "God of all comfort" to others whose struggles mirror our own. Our perspective about trials and suffering changes when we remember that our Savior is well acquainted with suffering. Our suffering is only a tiny taste of what our Lord went through when He carried the sins of humanity to the cross:

> Blessed be the God and Father of our Lord Jesus Christ, the Father of mercies and God of all comfort, who comforts us in all our affliction, so that we may be able to comfort those who are in any affliction, with the comfort with which we ourselves are comforted by God. For as we share abundantly in Christ's sufferings, so through Christ we share abundantly in comfort too. (2 Cor. 1:3–5)

C. S. Lewis once said, "Hardships often prepare ordinary people for an extraordinary destiny."[6] How is God using your past struggles and heartaches to comfort and encourage others who are walking a similar road? Do you readily comfort others with the same comfort you have received? If you don't have an answer to that question, I daresay, you're holding out. God did His part. Now it's your turn to do yours. Pay it forward. Mercy always gives back.

COMING CLEAN

1. Do you struggle with being honest about trials you are experiencing?

2. Would you say your core group of Christian friends is more likely to engage in the pretender game or come clean about struggles they are experiencing? And are there levels of disclosure? How deep do you go?

3. Have you ever felt confused or angry with God when He didn't respond to a trial in the way you had hoped? Did you voice your frustrations to anyone at the time? If so, what kind of response did you receive?

4. Reread Romans 5:3–5. Can you think of trials you have experienced that have produced endurance that in turn produced character that eventually led to hope?

5. What are your feelings about the challenge set forth in James 1:2 to "count it all joy" when you experience various trials? Can you think of a time when you were able to do this? Explain.

6. Have you ever experienced a trial that left you in the desert place? What did moving on look like for you?

7. Do you agree with the C. S. Lewis quote, "Hardships often prepare ordinary people for an extraordinary destiny"? Have you

experienced this in your own life? If so, describe how. If not, how might you use your past or current struggles to pay it forward and demonstrate the "God of all comfort" to someone else going through a similar situation?

Chapter 3

Us and Them

I like your Christ, I do not like your Christians.
Your Christians are so unlike your Christ.

—Mahatma Gandhi

I attended church less than ten times during my growing-up years. When I did, it was usually the result of an invitation to tag along Sunday morning after spending the night with a friend on a Saturday night. Such was the case one weekend during my sixth-grade year. My new best friend invited me to spend the night on a Saturday night. She attended church regularly, so I was instructed to pack my church clothes and Bible. I enthusiastically packed the children's Bible my grandparents had given me for Christmas when I was ten years old.

When I got to my friend's house, she told me she had to work on memorizing the names of the books of the Bible before Sunday school the next morning. In hindsight, I suppose, it was some sort of confirmation process to approve the youth for membership in the church. Her mother suggested that we both work together to memorize the books and offered a bit of incentive to me directly: "Vicki, since you don't have a church, maybe you can become a member at our church!" Or something to that effect. All I caught was the word *member.* (I should have clued in on the word *maybe.*) This was my shot to be able to say I belonged to a church. I had no idea how I would get there every week, but I would find a way. First things first.

My friend and I must have stayed up most of that night memorizing the books of the Bible. Sunday morning arrived, and I was anxious to get the quiz over with before the newly memorized books escaped my short-term memory. I recall each student being called out into the hall one at a time to rattle off the books. I continued to rehearse them in my head until I heard my name called. Finally it was my turn and I joined one of the teachers in the hallway. Just as I was about to begin, the teacher leaned down and cupped one of her hands around my shoulder. In a soft voice, she politely told me that I would not be able to participate in the drill because my parents were not "members of the church."

I was mortified. Humiliated. Heartbroken. I tucked my feelings deep inside and tried to play it cool when I walked back into the classroom. That morning, I walked away with a clear picture of us and them. The members and the visitors. Those who belonged to the club and those who didn't.

If at First You Don't Succeed . . .

A couple of years later, when I was in middle school, I gave church another shot. I recall talking my parents into taking my brother and me to Sunday school and church. My mother chose a beautiful church that was set along a meticulously landscaped road in an affluent part of Dallas. We had driven by it many times before, and she had always admired the white stucco finish accented by stained glass windows and a towering steeple. I would have preferred the popular Methodist church where my friends attended, but I was in no position to be picky. I was just thankful to be going, and announced to all my friends that I was going to church with my family on Sunday. It felt good just to be able to say that sentence out loud.

As we pulled into the parking lot of the church on Sunday morning, I remember feeling anxious about walking into a class where I wouldn't know a single person. Eighth-grade girls didn't go to the bathroom without a buddy, so this was a big stretch for me. Once in the classroom, the teacher introduced me to a couple of girls who offered up a courtesy smile and motioned to a seat next to them. Then they went back to the business of being BFFs. I was invisible. I'm pretty certain the only word spoken to me on that morning was when the teacher thanked me for coming as I was leaving. Funny, as we drove away the church didn't seem nearly as beautiful as when we had arrived. The towering steeple and stained glass windows did little to ward off the chill inside its walls.

The only time I entered a church after that was for an occasional weekend youth activity. It's hard to pass up an opportunity to play pass-the-lifesaver-on-a-toothpick when you knew a high percentage of the cute boys in your grade were going to be there. Fortunately, I wasn't denied admittance to the youth group activities due to a lack of membership credentials. Other than a few random weekend youth events, God rarely made a blip on the radar in my busy high school years. Except for maybe an occasional sleepover, where God-talk was common fare around 3:00 a.m., when all conversation pertaining to our current crushes had been exhausted and everyone was good and loopy, and you could usually count on one of the girls to bring up God. It didn't take long before someone else would declare that only "Christians" go to heaven and everyone else is bound for h-e-double-hockey-sticks, where the worm never dies and the furnace is set on high. No flannel board needed for that visual.

Of course, this served only to confuse me more. Bottom line: we were all up to the same stuff. Gossip. Backstabbing. Drinking. Fooling around with our boyfriends. Stealing hall passes off the teacher's desk when there was a substitute. And I was supposed to believe that these "punch-card Christians" were headed to paradise and I, once again, would be denied admittance at the pearly gates? Because why, exactly? And that was the problem. No one bothered to explain what exactly it meant to be a Christian. Bits and pieces, maybe. But not the whole story.

No Turning Back

Fast-forward several years. I was a junior in college and an ex-boyfriend-turned-friend invited me (along with my roommate) to a Christian event for college students over Labor Day weekend. I was weary from the party scene and figured it couldn't hurt to spend a weekend in a more wholesome environment than my normal weekend hangouts, so I accepted. When my roommate and I arrived at the retreat, it was overwhelming. There were several hundred college students milling around a retreat facility set on a beautiful lake property on the outskirts of Austin.

We met up with my ex-boyfriend, and he introduced us to his roommate and several of his friends. Everyone was so friendly. We stuck close by his group and attended a few breakout sessions and a recreation time that followed; then dinner was served before the Friday evening main session. I remember marveling at the cafeteria scene of various clusters of students gathered at the tables buzzing about who knows what. I hadn't spent much time with Jesus people before, and I suppose I was imagining something different. Laughter echoed throughout the room as they enjoyed the company of one another. They seemed so comfortable. Relaxed. And why not? This was clearly a familiar environment to them. This was their comfort zone. I wondered if this is what it had been like for my high school friends who attended weekend retreats and Christian summer camps.

I marveled at the fact that it was Labor Day weekend and they could be at any number of parties being held on campus. But they chose to be here. No alcohol. No drunken revelry. I wondered how it was that they didn't need that to fit in, to have fun. I was admittedly burned-out from the weekend party scene, but at the same time, it still had a pull on me. Maybe because it was all I knew. It was *my* comfort zone. I glanced at my watch. On a typical weekend, I would be getting ready for another weekend of parties and club hopping with my friends. They would be shocked if they could see me sitting in a campground dining hall with the Jesus people. They would never let me live it down. *What was I doing here?* It just didn't add up. I felt strangely like the outsider who had been granted temporary admittance with a weekend pass. And it was about to get real interesting.

I noticed a flurry of activity as the students around me began to get up and unload their trays. Apparently, it was time to head to the Friday evening main session. Everyone seemed to know the drill. My roommate and I followed suit as if we, too, had done this countless times before.

For the most part the evening session was a blur, until the worship leader got up to play a few closing songs. I don't remember what the main speaker talked about that night, but I remember the worship leader's story as he strummed his guitar. He shared how, for years, he had attempted to fill the empty places in his heart with everything the world had to offer. Parties. Alcohol. Drugs. Sex. He was telling my story. I tuned in and clung to his every word. He wrapped it up by sharing how a friend sat him down and told him about the love of Christ and His grace and forgiveness. He mentioned that he felt like God had been chasing him and it was time to slow down. To be caught. The worship leader then invited the students to make the same decision.

Finally, for the first time, I heard the gospel clearly. No more bits and pieces. I learned that belonging to a beautiful church with a towering steeple and pretty stained glass windows won't save you. Salvation isn't promised to those who are born into families who faithfully punch their cards on Sunday morning. Nor is it gained by those who can successfully recite the books of the Bible and have a certificate to show for it on Judgment Day. As the worship leader unpacked the gospel message that night, the beautiful love story of redemption invaded my heart, and I felt a peace that's hard to describe, even to this day. "For God so loved the world [everyone, not just the church kids], that he gave his only Son [a sacrifice for undeserving sinners; for me. He meets us where we are. Penalty paid.], that whoever believes in him should not perish but have eternal life" (John 3:16). New life. That sounded so good. Almost too good to be true. The worship leader began to play a song. With my head bowed, I found myself conversing silently with this God I wasn't sure had even existed the day before. I needed this grace. My sin list had grown quite long. On about the eleventh stanza of "I Have Decided to Follow Jesus," I gave up the chase.

A New Beginning

The first couple of years after I dumped my baggage at the foot of the cross could best be described as a sprint. I didn't just walk away a new creation, I ran with the Good News. I couldn't get enough of God's Word. I read, reread, memorized, and highlighted. I soaked up the Bible like a sponge. Before I knew it, I could hold my weight in my college Sunday school class with most of my peers who grew up going to church. I could turn to the correct book in the Bible as quickly as these Bible-drill alumni, without having to take a quick peek at the table of contents. And I actively shared my faith with anyone who was willing to listen. And even those who weren't. (I've since had to go back and apologize to a few of my family members for my overzealous conversion tactics during those first few years. My presentation wasn't always pretty, even if my motives were pure.) I hit the ground running, fueled by a grateful heart and a radically changed life. I sincerely wanted everyone to experience God's grace and forgiveness.

But then life began to happen. I married less than two years after becoming a Christian. Ironically, I met my husband at the same college event where I met Jesus. Yep, I met my Prince and my Prince Charming on the same day. In addition to being the most handsome guy I had ever laid eyes upon, he possessed a godliness and wisdom beyond his years. Within three months of being married, we discovered we were expecting a child. By our six-year anniversary, we would have a newborn, a toddler, a kindergartner, a two-story house, a dog, and a minivan (the one car I swore I'd never drive). Life got crazy. Really fast. I would learn that the Christian journey is a marathon, not a sprint. Some days you make more progress than others. Like the days when you're a single college student taking a twelve-hour course load and your biggest worry of the day is whether or not to order takeout from Pizza Hut or Domino's.

Us . . .

With a husband and three kids to tend to, my biggest worry in this new chapter of my life was survival. Like it or not, I was forced to take my pace down a notch. My sprint became a slow, exhausted jog with many breaks on the sidelines—if you consider *Sesame Street* and *Barney* a break. Welcome to life in the suburban fast lane. The more entrenched I became in my Christian comfort zone, the less focused I became on the world outside my door. Let's be honest, "go and make disciples" gets lost in a sea of potty training, math drill cards, peewee soccer, and cutting coupons that will probably never make it into your purse. Somewhere along the way, the tyranny of the urgent takes first place. You don't plan for it to happen. It just does. And before you know it, sharing the Good News becomes just another chore on the to-do list. Assuming it makes the list.

But I've learned—the hard way—that when we fail to reflect back on the power of the cross in our own lives, we cease to be effective when it comes to pointing others to the cross. In my early years as a new believer, I went through several evangelism training programs. I was actively sharing my faith, but for the most part, I was doing it out of a sense of obligation. Good Christians go through evangelism training programs, right? Good Christians share their faith. Good Christians attend church-wide visitation. Please know that I'm not knocking evangelism training programs, but for me, it would have been far more effective had I funneled my energy into simply sharing my own before-and-after story—my sinful state before the cross and my radically changed life after the cross. I had come to rely on a formula rather than simply telling my story from the heart. And the cross faded into the background.

Perhaps the most dangerous outcome of our failure to consistently reflect on the power of the cross is that it births a prideful arrogance in our hearts, making it easy for Christianity to become a members-only club where we see the world through a lens of us and them. At some point it becomes uncomfortable to be around them. Have you ever felt that? Let's be honest, I think all of us have. So strange, isn't it? You and I *were* them before encountering Christ's forgiveness. And then over time, instead of maintaining a humble and compassionate heart toward the lost, we become pharisaical, slowly adding individuals and groups of people to our *them* quarantine list.

The them who vote differently than our Christian clique at election time.

The them who believe certain things are acceptable, even though the Bible clearly puts them in the no-zone.

The them who refuse to believe life begins at conception or prefer to sleep in on Sunday mornings.

The them who support same-sex marriage or sex education in grade school.

Ouch. When it comes to loving our neighbors, the church has much room for improvement. Kindness is easy to pull off when the recipient is among those in the *us* group. Our posse. Our peeps. Our kind.

And at some point along the way in my busy suburban life, I became comfortable in my Christian cocoon as part of the us group. I failed to remember that I had once been part of them. Besides, I had a duty to raise my children in the faith and protect them from non-Christian influences, right? I voiced a concern for them, but it was often in a self-righteous and judgmental tone. *Bless their hearts; they need Jesus, but do me a favor, and stay on your side of the fence, and I'll stay on mine, mm-kay?*

As I look back, the division into us and them was all very gradual. It was more of a slow, spiritual choking over the years as my priorities had shifted. One day, I realized I had become the very person who had turned me off to Christianity in my pre-cross days. I weep as I type those words. It's not easy to digest, but it needs to be said.

. . . And Them

It was a steamy hot Sunday afternoon in Austin, Texas. And by "steamy hot," I mean 107 degrees with zero breeze. On this particular Fourth of July weekend in 2004, my family joined other members from our church on the steps of our state capitol for a rally sponsored by a Christian organization. The event was called a "Declaration of Dependence" and was organized for the purpose of rallying support among Texans to vote for a proposition that would define marriage solely as a union between a man and a woman. The theme, "Declaration of Dependence," served as a reminder that our highest goal is dependence on a holy God. Our pastor had encouraged the congregation to attend the event if possible, so we packed up the kids in the car and decided to brave the sweltering heat.

I'm not sure what I was expecting when I got to the rally, but I remember being surprised at the large number of protesters. There were two groups. One was from a well-known civil rights organization that, according to their website, supports causes related to advancing homosexuality through "relentless non-violent resistance."[1] They were represented by a couple hundred people in matching T-shirts standing together to the left of the capitol steps. The other group—the Christians who had shown up to support the proposition—numbered about the same and stood to the right of the capitol steps. *Us* and *them*.

The event began with a few familiar hymns and worship choruses. Many in the large group of protesters on the left sang the words and some even raised their hands in worship. That was my first shock. What was going on here? How did they know these songs? These were our songs. I was seriously confused. There was also another group of protesters—a handful of angry individuals. Suffice it to say, they weren't interested in singing Jesus songs. And it was hot, which probably made them even crankier. They planted themselves front and center during the worship and began to yell obscenities toward our group. At one point, two gay men even stepped up onto the capitol steps and began making out in front of the crowd in an attempt to incite members from our group.

At this point I was seriously second-guessing our decision to bring our children to the rally. They were sixteen, fourteen, and eleven years old, and by default of living in Austin, they were certainly no strangers to occasional same-sex public displays of affection. Let's just say that this display went well beyond affection. The us and them just got a little more clearly defined, or so I thought. I was feeling pretty self-righteous, standing among my brigade of onward-Christian-soldiers. When the time of singing ended, the keynote speaker began to address the crowd. He emphasized the importance of supporting the proposition and was met with more heckling from the small group of angry protesters. At that time some of the peaceful protesters from the larger group approached the individuals and politely asked them to stop. And something within my heart stirred. The other side—the them group—interceded on our behalf. First the hymns, and now this.

It was then that I felt a clear put-me-completely-out-of-my-comfort-zone nudging from God. He made it crystal clear that I was to go stand with them. Not in support of them, but simply to be with them. Panic. But then there was a peace. *No, this is right. I don't completely understand it—my* us *friends will probably question my sanity, but this is right.* So I announced to my family that I was going to venture over to the large group of protesters, which was met with confused Mom-has-completely-lost-it stares. Before I could chicken out, I turned and walked away from my comfort zone. Goodbye, us. Hello, them.

I made my way into the center of the crowd of protesters and ended up standing behind two women with a baby in an umbrella stroller. Now what? I had no idea. The baby was fussy because, well, did I mention it was 107 degrees? There was not a tree nearby to offer even a sliver of shade to the crowd. One of the women picked up the baby and began to alternate between blowing in her face and fanning her face with her hand. It was clear they were concerned about the baby getting too hot. Having lived in Austin for over two decades, I held in my hand the answer to their dilemma— one of those spray water bottles with a tiny battery-operated fan blade attached to the nozzle. Trust me, anyone in Texas with kids who play outdoor sports owns a half dozen of these jewels. I tapped one of the women gently on the shoulder and stammered nervously, "Would you like to use this to spray your baby?" The woman took one look at my unusual offering and kindly replied, "Do you mind?" And with that, the ice broke. As the keynote speaker continued in the backdrop, we exchanged pleasantries about the weather and, of course, their adorable, but very hot, baby girl.

As we talked, I couldn't help but glance around at the crowd of protesters. Funny thing, as I stood among them rather than across from them, I became more aware of our similarities, not our differences. There was no distinguishing factor that made them stand out as different from those in my group. We were all dressed similarly. We were all desperately hot. We were all frantically fanning ourselves. And, truth be told, we were all probably second-guessing the decision to leave the comfort of our air-conditioned homes on a day when the temperature soared past 100 degrees. As I took in the scene from this new vantage point, I began to see people, not protesters. People in need of a Savior, just like me.

Minutes later the rally came to a close. The women, who were now holding a happy, freshly spritzed baby, thanked me profusely as they handed back the spray water bottle. We bantered for a bit more, and then one of the women asked if I was with a part of their group. This question was not unusual, given I was one of the few standing among them without a matching T-shirt sporting their group logo. "No, actually, my family is over there," I said, pointing off to the right. They were a bit shocked at the realization that I wasn't one of them, but there was no judgment in their expression. And then without even thinking, I said, "Listen, I want to tell you something. I'm so very sorry for the way many Christians—myself included—have treated you in the past. I just want you to know that." *Whew, I said it. And it felt really good.*

Never in a million years could I have predicted the reply that followed when one of the women replied, "You know, we're sorry too—about the radical protesters that showed up today and said some hurtful things to your group. We want you to know they don't represent us." And with that, we did what came naturally and embraced in a quick group hug. There was no need to serve up a litany of Bible verses or engage them in a theological debate in an effort to convince them of their sin and apparent need of a Savior. Nor was there a need to offer a disclaimer that neither my comment nor my hug were endorsements of their lifestyle. We knew where the other stood when it came to our beliefs on this topic. Until that day, I had stood at a distance and talked *about* them. In obeying God's nudge and taking a few steps out of my comfort zone, I experienced the blessing of talking *with* them.

As I walked away from the rally, I had a change of heart over how I would interact with them in the future. The truth is Jesus didn't command us with His final words in Mark 16:15 to go into the world and legislate morality. He instructed us to "go into all the world and proclaim the gospel." He, too, lived in immoral times, but it was never His focus to rally the government to adopt a moral, Christian code. I'm not suggesting we adopt an attitude of "who cares?" when it comes to our laws. I'm merely suggesting we make it our primary focus to love others with the power of the gospel, rather than change policy. Like Jesus did.

We

I'm no stranger to the role of the outcast. I've played that part before. Skeletons were tumbling out of the closet by the time I finally embraced Christ's forgiveness back in 1985. I didn't end up at the cross because someone pointed a finger in my face and told me I had broken the rules. Oh, there were a few who attempted that strategy over the years, but their judgment drove me only further away. When I think back on my own journey, it was the beauty of the gospel that drew me to Him: "Or do you think lightly of the riches of His kindness and tolerance and patience, not knowing that the kindness of God leads you to repentance?" (Rom. 2:4 NASB). It was His kindness that led me to repentance. His redemption, not the rules.

Jesus was no stranger to the outcasts and "the least of these" (Matt. 25:40). The woman caught in adultery. Zacchaeus. The Samaritan woman. He hung out with a colorful list of sinners and misfits. His comfort zone was simply wherever the gospel was needed at the moment. He'd talk to anyone who would listen. He preferred the them crowd over the us crowd on the majority of days in His three-year earthly ministry. In fact, He had more than a few choice words for the us crowd and their hypocritical finger-pointing habit—criticism that would probably get Him ushered out of most churches today. But when it comes to extending genuine kindness to others, He is our ultimate role model. He looked beneath the deed and saw the need.

As I've matured in my faith over the past several years and grown more and more aware of my own depravity, the chasm between us and them has begun to close. *They* don't need Jesus—we *all* need Jesus. *They* are not sinners. We *all* are sinners. Sin is not a behavior—it is a condition. We all need the good news that God, in His unmatched kindness, sent His Son to die for us. All of us. It's time to do away with this silly notion of us and them and begin to see ourselves as part of a collective *we*.

COMING CLEAN

1. When you think of the concept of us and them, what comes to mind? Have you ever felt like *them*? Explain.

2. In what ways do you currently venture outside of your Christian comfort zone to bridge the gap between us and them? How might you need to change in this area?

3. If you take an honest look at your attitude toward them, is it one of finger-pointing and judgment or kindness and compassion? Explain.

4. Describe some of the emotions you were feeling when you read about my experience at the rally. If God had nudged your heart to stand among the other group, would you have been obedient? Explain.

5. When you think about the term *them*, who comes to mind? (Examples: those in other faiths; those who vote differently from you; the homeless; the tattooed and pierced.) In what ways might God be nudging your heart to stand among them? What might a first step in that direction look like for you?

Chapter 4

Unclaimed Baggage

Help me to find in his death the reality and
immensity of his love. Open for me the wondrous
volumes of truth in his, "It is finished."

—PURITAN PRAYER, *The Valley of Vision: A*
Collection of Puritan Prayers and Devotions

It was 1995. I stood alone in a small Sunday school room at a church in Houston, Texas. I was petrified yet excited about the breakout session I was scheduled to teach at a large women's conference in half an hour. I stared blankly at the rows of empty chairs and wondered if it would be less intimidating to stack some of the chairs in a corner and have fewer rows. I wasn't anticipating many attendees at this particular breakout session.

You see, I had taught on many topics before, but they were always in the *safe* zone. Feel-good topics. The kinds that make you smile and laugh and feel warm and toasty inside when you leave—God's grace, understanding your child's temperament, the art of being a good friend, that sort of thing. Topics like that were always well attended, and I was given a big room to justify the crowd. But if my instincts were correct, there would be no large crowd today. This breakout might not be popular or well attended, but it had a greater potential to change lives than all the other breakouts I'd taught in the past—combined. I was going to speak on a topic that I had boldly told God was off-limits for the first ten years I was a believer.

I was going to recount a sin that had occurred fifteen years prior—one that left me with such a burden of shame that I did not speak of it to a single soul for several years. When I became a Christian in my college years, I could hardly believe the good news that a sin this big was forgiven. I left it at the foot of the cross that day, but I eventually picked it back up and the shame that came with it. I've often taught that if you don't check your baggage at the foot of the cross, the enemy will be glad to deliver it to your doorstep, and that's exactly what happened to me. Not dealing with my sin and shame manifested itself in a variety of dysfunctional behaviors that eventually led me to get some professional Christian counseling where, with God's help, my road to healing finally began.

As I finished rearranging the chairs, the women began to trickle into the breakout room. Some wore blank expressions that hinted at unresolved grief. Others averted their eyes and looked for a seat on the back row. I'm sure it had taken every ounce of courage to enter the room, and they wanted to make sure there was a quick getaway just in case it was more than they could bear. I understood. I wore the same expression for many years. But I was done with pretending. The Good News was just too good not to share.

My Story

I was barely seventeen when I sat in the waiting room of an abortion clinic. No one knew I was pregnant, except my boyfriend and a coworker who had recommended the clinic. I was pro-choice by default of the fact that my parents were pro-choice, so this decision had been a no-brainer. I was a junior in high school, popular among my peers, and on the varsity cheerleading squad. I had aspirations to attend college after graduation. A baby certainly wouldn't fit within those plans. My boyfriend seemed to struggle more with the decision than I did, finding it difficult to reconcile this choice with his Catholic upbringing. However, he agreed there was no other practical solution. He was a graduating senior and had been awarded an athletic scholarship at a nearby university. We called the clinic and felt relieved when a date was on the calendar.

My boyfriend normally drove me to school, so my parents didn't suspect a thing when he pulled into the driveway on that morning in November. Little was said during the twenty-mile drive to the clinic on the outskirts of town. He seemed to be focused on the directions to make sure that we didn't get lost. I fumbled with the radio, looking for anything to distract me from thinking about the *procedure*. I couldn't bring myself to say the word—even in my mind. Finally we arrived at the clinic. As we entered the waiting room, I noticed several other girls who appeared to be close to my age, some alone and a few with their boyfriends. There was another girl who was clearly much younger, sitting stoically next to her mother. I wondered for a moment about their stories. I checked in at the window and was immediately handed a mound of paperwork. My boyfriend settled the bill, paying $250 in cash. After filling out the required forms, we passed the time by playing hangman and tic-tac-toe on a scratch sheet of paper. The time spent in the waiting room seemed like an eternity when, in actuality, it was less than a half hour.

I was startled when the nurse standing in the doorway called my name. I stood and briefly looked back at my boyfriend. He gave me a gentle nod of reassurance as I walked toward the nurse. I didn't look back again as I walked through the doorway and was ushered down a narrow corridor. After a blood test and a brief meeting with a nurse to confirm my decision to move forward with the procedure, I was led into a cold and sterile room. The details after that are a blur, gray and devoid of detail. A brief introduction by a doctor in a white lab coat. A friendly nurse who held my hand as the anesthesia was administered. And then nothing.

My next memory is of waking up in a larger room with many beds, each closed off by curtains. I was alone for a few minutes until a nurse came to my side and informed me that I was in recovery. The nurse asked me if I had brought anyone with me and if I would like that person to join me in the recovery room. I nodded my head and softly gave my boyfriend's name. I was not in any pain, but my mind was racing. I began to cry softly. I didn't want to call attention to myself, so I tried to muffle my sobs by turning my head into my pillow. I had thought I would feel nothing but sheer relief, so the tears caught me off guard. When I looked up, my boyfriend was at my side. He seemed uncertain about how to respond to my sadness. He fidgeted nervously and leaned down and whispered, "We'll be out of here soon." His words brought little comfort, and I remember just wanting my mother. I was seventeen years old, and I needed my mother. But my mother didn't know. We had agreed not to tell anyone. In fact, we agreed to never mention the procedure or acknowledge this day again.

Unfortunately, moving on wasn't as easy as I had imagined. In spite of being very pro-choice at the time, I couldn't seem to reconcile the guilt that would plague me from time to time when the memory resurfaced.

Laying It Down

Four years later I would lay that sin at the foot of the cross, desperate for God's mercy and forgiveness. While my sin list was a long one, the abortion was at the top when it came to my most grievous sins. It played a huge part in driving me to the cross and admitting my need for a Savior. The abortion was foremost in my mind that evening when I bowed my head and gave up the chase. I welcomed this forgiveness and new life that were being offered. If God could forgive me, then maybe, just maybe, I could forgive myself.

I felt a tremendous weight had been lifted off me when I laid that burden down. The feeling was indescribable. In that moment I understood what it meant to share the good news of God's love and forgiveness. I was on the receiving end of that good news and couldn't wait to share it with others. Only one problem: I quickly discovered that God's people weren't as willing to talk about their own messy moments when they encountered God's redemptive grace. Those moments were always referenced in second- or third-person: you, he, she, his, her, they, their. But never in first person. When talking about the messiness of life and faith, words like *I*, *me*, and *my* were often far too personal and revealing.

Picking It Back Up

Shortly after becoming a Christian, I was in my new college Sunday school class when the topic of abortion came up. "Abortion is murder," chimed one girl in a Laura Ashley puff-sleeved dress with matching hair bow—the standard Sunday-morning uniform for an eighties college girl in the Bible Belt. Her comment was met with a chorus of nods and affirmations by most of the other girls in our group. Another girl piled on, "I mean, if it's murder, the women having them should do jail time." And that was the moment I made the decision to never, never, ever speak in detail about my past. God may have set me free, but His people were ready to lock me up.

After a while I began to notice a pattern when the topic of abortion would come up. Finger-pointing and judgments flowed freely with little concern that people's words might apply to anyone in their group. And why would they? The underlying assumption was that no one in the church would do such a thing. Even those of us who arrived a little late to the party. It was those *other* people—*them*. As a new believer I desperately wanted to fit in with my new family—my brothers and sisters in Christ—which meant I was left with one option when it came to dealing with and healing from my past sin of abortion (and other sins on the list, I might add): get a Laura Ashley puff-sleeved dress and shut my mouth. As a bonus, I would also buy a matching quilted Bible cover. That would throw them off. At least for a while.

Out of the Darkness

I was a new bride of about a month when I dumped the news of my past abortion on my husband. I don't recall what precipitated the decision to come clean with him, but I'm sure it was the result of pressure building up from the guilt I had carried alone for so many years. There was a crack in the dam that night and, bless his heart, he had little warning of the impending flood to come. He knew I wasn't a virgin when we married, but I didn't give him much detail beyond that. I came very close to telling him on several occasions during our engagement, but I always chickened out.

I was tormented by the fact that he didn't know everything, but I was desperately afraid I might lose him. He had saved himself for a quarter of a century, and I already felt like he was getting the short end of the stick in marrying the non-virgin girl. I clearly didn't give him enough credit because when I burst into tears and told him one month into our marriage, he wrapped his arms around me and said, "You're forgiven." And he meant it. Unfortunately, we wouldn't talk about it again until seven years later, when we found ourselves sitting next to each other in a counselor's office.

We landed in that counselor's office due to some other issues, but the abortion came up early in our sessions. I confessed that I didn't feel like my puritan husband deserved a wife with such a tainted past and he was only sticking around because he had to. Once we worked through that pain and my husband reassured me that was not the case, I began to take steps toward healing from the shame of the abortion. I was finally free to talk about it with my very best friend. And, in his defense, he would have talked about it sooner, but I had made it clear that it was off-limits after the original confession.

That day in the counselor's office, talking about the abortion felt like I had crept up to the attic of my soul and carried out the dusty lockbox containing my shameful secret. I brought it out of the darkness and exposed it to the light.

I was no longer content to allow my unclaimed baggage to remain on the carousel of shame for another day. With the help and encouragement of my counselor and with my husband by my side, I turned the key on the dusty lockbox and slowly opened the lid. For several weeks we unpacked that lockbox of sin and shame. For the first time, I recounted the details of that day. I laid my soul bare, and I held nothing back. I mourned the loss of life—what was to be my first child. I wept over the fact that a young seventeen-year-old girl had to make the decision virtually alone, and even worse, she had to hide the aftermath of grief that followed. I grieved every harsh and judgmental word that had been spoken by my very own brothers and sisters in Christ and the pressure I had felt to continue hiding the sin in spite of the fact that Christ had set me free. I grieved the collateral damage it had indirectly had on my family in my refusal to address the sin and accept God's forgiveness. Every step of the way, God met me in my grief.

Into the Light

Another step in my healing process came when I initiated a coffee date with each of my three closest friends for the purpose of sharing about my past abortion. I wanted their support and prayers in regard to my decision to travel and speak on the topic and the good news of God's forgiveness. My counselor had shared that there is great power in confessing a sin to a trusted friend because it reduces the shame and condemnation that is often associated with a secret sin. God's Word supports her counsel: "Therefore, confess your sins to one another and pray for one another, that you may be healed" (James 5:16). It is healing to confess a sin to someone (assuming she is a trustworthy and mature believer), acknowledge the remorse, and more important, celebrate the forgiveness. Beth Moore writes: "Confession silences the taunts of our accuser, makes our hearts clean, and makes our souls well."[1]

I met individually with each of my friends over a two-week period and, in victory, shared about my past. Each one listened intently as I asked for her prayers regarding the upcoming events. I asked them to pray specifically that God would set women free from their sin and shame. Would you believe that each of my three friends confessed that they, too, had experienced abortions in their pasts and were suffering in silent shame? God certainly confirmed the need to bring this topic out into the open. How sad that each of us had been suffering alone over the same sin when we could have been such a support to one another! The enemy had certainly gotten a victory in persuading us to remain silent, convinced we were the only ones with such horrific sin in our pasts. We as believers cannot be effective in offering others hope and forgiveness when we're not living in the light of that hope. Hearing my friends' confessions left me with an even stronger resolve to bring God's message of forgiveness to my Christian sisters.

The next three years of traveling and teaching about finding forgiveness after abortion were pivotal in my life. I could write an entire book based on the stories I heard from women while on the road. The description for the breakout noted that it was for women who had experienced an abortion or those who wanted to help someone dear to them who had had an abortion in her past. Many women would pull me aside after the breakout and share they had told their friends they were attending to "help a friend," when in fact they were there for themselves. Some women were too ashamed to walk through the doors and would find me later to ask if I had extra copies of notes or handouts.

I spoke to a pastor's wife who attended the breakout with a hurting friend, but the wife whispered in my ear that she, too, had had an abortion. She was too ashamed to tell the friend with her. And then there was the pastor's wife who was beside herself with grief. She confided that she and her husband slipped up during their engagement and discovered she was pregnant. Her husband was in seminary at the time and insisted she have an abortion since it would affect his future dream of becoming a pastor. Years later he was the senior pastor at a large church and respected by many in his congregation. Unfortunately, he lost the respect of his wife in the process. She was angry and bitter beyond belief.

I reminded the women in my sessions that God has forgiven our sins "as far as the east is from the west" (Ps. 103:12). When He cried out on the cross, "It is finished," He didn't add a footnote with a list of exceptions to His declaration. To doubt God's forgiveness, in a sense, says, "My sin is just too big for Your forgiveness, Lord. But thanks all the same. I'll pass on this forgiveness You are offering." Philippians 3:13–14 says, "Brothers, I do not consider that I have made it my own. But one thing I do: forgetting what lies behind and straining forward to what lies ahead, I press on toward the goal for the prize of the upward call of God in Christ Jesus." The Greek word for *forgetting* is *ĕpilanthanŏmai*, which means to "lose out of mind; to neglect."[2] Try as we may, some sins we will never be able to "lose out of mind." Oh, that it were possible!

Healing comes when we learn to ignore the accuser's shameful reminders of our past sins. In doing so, shame loses the power of control in our lives. I shared with the women in the breakout session that it's normal to visit our past sins from time to time, but we don't have to pack a bag and stay overnight. We certainly don't have to make our home with them. The only positive outcome in reflecting back on a past sin is to remember what God has done. Period. It is not for the purpose of beating up ourselves and feeling shame but rather to remind us of God's grace and mercy.

It is finished.

There is no sin too big for the grace of God. Promiscuity? It is finished. Addictions? It is finished. Adultery? It is finished.

I remember a commitment time at a large women's event where I shared this hope. A woman approached me for prayer but broke down in sobs as she said, "This Jesus could never forgive my sin." She proceeded to whisper in my ear, "I killed my unborn baby doing crack cocaine." I wrapped my arms around this sweet woman and then looked her in the eye and firmly told her, "It is finished."

The more I write and speak to women's groups, the more convinced I become that far too many women are living in the past, defined by their sin, rather than being defined by God's grace in the present. And let's be honest. We're not just talking about the past. Nor are we talking about just the big sins. Even the smallest of sins can define us if we allow it to. We will continue to sin in our journeys from the cross to the finish line. Putting the past behind us is the result not of forgetting our past sins, but rather of remembering their place on the cross. We can't move forward until we decide to forget the past—whether it was an act committed years ago, months ago, yesterday, or just minutes ago. Mind you, you probably won't completely forget, because it simply isn't possible. Rather, as we move forward, we do so with a vision of our sins nailed to the cross in our rearview mirror. "Those who belong to Christ Jesus have nailed the passions and desires of their sinful nature to his cross and crucified them there" (Gal. 5:24 NLT). It's time to leave the shackles of your sins at the foot of the cross. You are no longer bound by them. It is finished.

Repurposed for a Purpose

I love scouring antique shops and finding long-forgotten items that can be given a new life, repurposed in my home. One of my favorites is a mantel that was salvaged from an old farmhouse; it now hangs in a guest bedroom. Another favorite is a solid-wood exterior door that is more than one hundred years old. It still contains the original mouth-blown glass inset. I would rather find an antique item with a story behind it and give it a second life than pay more for something that is polished and new but lacks both character and a backstory. (And probably costs more!)

One of my all-time favorite repurposed items is a gift I recently received from a pastor and his wife. I had the blessing of meeting the wife last year in the midst of a rather tumultuous storm she and her husband were experiencing. Her husband was guilty of an infidelity, and God allowed me to play a small part in their restoration process by recommending a wonderful Christian counselor. Fortunately, her husband responded with brokenness over his sin—the kind of brokenness that leads to a godly sorrow and repentance (2 Cor. 7:10).

During this time of restoration, God had taken him to the woodshop. And when I say "woodshop," I mean it literally. He is a very talented wood craftsman and made me a beautiful wood lap desk as a thank-you gift. In the note he and his wife attached to the desk, he explained that the lap desk was created from two-hundred-year-old heart pine from a historic home in Mobile, Alabama. The home was being restored, and the old wood was destined to end up in a trash heap. He reclaimed the wood and repurposed it into something useful. What a beautiful picture of what God, the great Carpenter, is doing this very minute in his life. In my life. In your life. The note said, "I just wanted to say thank you for believing that 'old things' can become 'new' again."

I believe old things can become new again because I've been that old thing. God, in His mercy, has reclaimed my life from the trash heap—not once, not twice, but many times over. Repurposed for His glory. Redeemed by His love. And I've never, ever been the same.

Repurposed lives are passionate about repurposing other lives. I don't deserve a thank you for that. I am simply passing along what I myself have experienced firsthand during my time in the woodshop. Every time I see that lap desk sitting on the ottoman of my favorite writing chair, I am reminded that God takes His children to the woodshop—not behind the woodshed for a spiritual beat down. Oh, the years I wasted sitting in the woodshed with my head ducked in shame! God didn't put me there. I put myself there. Lives are never repurposed in the woodshed. Jesus took the licks for us, so why do we go there? Or, even worse, send others there when they mess up?

Leaving the Woodshed

What's your story? Is there an area of your past that, up until now, you've kept in hiding? Let me ask you this: Are you free? If you are truly free, you won't be able to shut up about the One who set you free. When you encounter someone who has experienced a similar story as yours, are you able to share about your own journey to freedom? If not, chances are very good that you're still in the woodshed, still bound up by that sin that Christ has already died to free you from. God is not there, so why do you stay? And if your picture of God involves Him being in the woodshed, you need to go back to the drawing board about who God really is. Or are you afraid to face the judgment of people who might wait on the other side of the woodshed door should you choose to walk out in liberation? I can't promise you those people don't exist, but I will tell you this little secret about them: they're in the woodshed too. If they were free, they would cheer you on, grab your hand, and drag you to the *woodshop*. You don't forget the taste of freedom. Ever.

Walk toward the woodshed door. Turn the knob. That's it, you can do it. Now, open the door and walk away. No, run away. Your Carpenter waits for you in the woodshop. He wants to take your messes and repurpose them for His glory and your joy. He wants to create something beautiful from the ashes.

Let your story of repurposing begin.

COMING CLEAN

1. I am going to ask you to do something difficult. When you think of the term *unclaimed baggage*, what are some past sins that have plagued you? I realize it may be hard for you to write them down. Abbreviate if you need to, but please don't allow your shame to cause you to walk away from this spiritual exercise. Putting something down in writing is a significant first step in admitting it, facing it, and getting it out in the open so you can begin the process of healing.

2. If you have never confessed your sins to a trusted Christian friend (James 5:16), I want you to consider doing so. I realize this is potentially dangerous, so I'd want you to be careful when it comes to choosing someone. Give it a lot of thought and prayer. It needs to be someone who is mature in the faith and trustworthy. I wouldn't ask you to do this unless I felt it was an important step.

3. Have you truly embraced Jesus' claim that "it is finished"? In other words, have you removed your unclaimed baggage from the carousel of shame and, with Christ's help, laid it at the foot of the cross? If not, what is holding you back?

4. Look back over the sins you listed in your answer to the first question. Beside each one write, "It is finished." Make an effort to claim that truth when the sins of your past come to mind.

5. How might God want to use your story (in the woodshop) as part of His bigger story? Will you let Him?

Chapter 5

Buried Alive

*Shame corrodes the very part of us that
believes we are capable of change.*

—Brené Brown

She was visibly shaking as she sat across from me at my
kitchen table. I scooted my chair closer to hers and reached
across the table and took her hand in mine.

"I want you to know something. There is absolutely no
sin that is too big for the forgiveness of Jesus Christ." Tears
pooled in her eyes as she looked up and met my glance.

"I want to believe that. I really do. But you don't know
what I've done."

She was nineteen years old, a freshman in college. She was
the suitemate of a friend's daughter, and I was meeting her

for the first time. Her long blonde hair swept back in a messy ponytail, she was a beautiful girl who likely had plenty of attention from the guys. I had just tucked my kids into bed when my friend's daughter called and asked if she could bring her suitemate over to talk. She explained that her friend was extremely upset about something that had happened over the weekend and had made several comments about "no longer wanting to live." My friend's daughter knew that I had a testimony that included some pretty wild years in high school and college and, for that reason, felt I would be a good person to minister to her suitemate. I was honored that she thought of me as a safe person to comfort her friend in such a fragile situation.

One look at the poor girl and it was clear she was buckling under the weight of shame. I knew the look because I'd been there before. Her head bowed, she fidgeted in her seat as she worked up her nerve to share the details that had led her to my doorstep. I squeezed her hand and told her I had all night if she needed it. There was no rush. She sniffled as I handed her a tissue and she began, "I'm a Christian and I was raised going to church. I should have known better." With every word, she seemed to get a tiny bit braver. "I used to judge the girls in high school that did stupid stuff like this. Now, I am *that girl*. Actually, I'm worse than that girl."

I interrupted, gently patting her hand. "Hey, you know what? You're in good company. I've been that girl too. I know exactly where you're coming from." And with that, the flood of tears began as she explained her situation. I listened as she recounted the night where her life had taken a drastic turn: two older boys were hitting on her and her roommate at a party;

lots of alcohol involved; an invitation to go back to the guys' apartment and watch a movie; more alcohol followed; sex with the boys and even a dare to kiss her roommate at the guys' prodding. Flattered by the guys' attention and in an altered state, reason and good judgment had left the party hours ago. She and her roommate succumbed to the boys' dare to kiss each other and eventually relented to their pleas to engage in group sex. As if the sex wasn't enough to deal with the following morning, she had to face her roommate every day that followed. It was a mess.

When she blurted out the last part of her story, it was as if she expelled her last ounce of courage along with those final words in her confession. Overcome by the weight of her shame, she reacted by covering her face with her hands. She softly sobbed, "I don't want to live anymore." My heart broke for her. By this point, I had scooted my chair directly in front of her. I leaned over, wrapping my arms tightly around her as if I was cradling one of my own children, and told her what she'd been taught in church all those years but perhaps had been words on a page until that moment: "You are loved by God, and you are forgiven."

Mercy meets us in our mess. Sometimes, we can't see Mercy because we're hiding behind our hands. So He waits.

Spiritual Bankruptcy

The dictionary defines *shame* as "the painful feeling arising from the consciousness of something dishonorable, improper, ridiculous, etc., done by oneself or another."[1] The earliest account of shame was felt in the immediate aftermath of Adam and Eve's sin in the garden. Prior to their sin, Scripture tells us they "were both naked and were not ashamed" (Gen. 2:25). One chapter later they are sewing fig leaves together and playing a game of hide-and-seek with God. With that one forbidden bite came man's first bitter taste of shame.

Mark Twain once said, "Man is the only animal that blushes—or needs to."[2] Whether we bring shame upon ourselves, or it enters our lives as an unwelcome intruder from circumstances beyond our control, the end result is the same. If not addressed, shame will devour us from the inside out. It short-circuits our true identity and hinders us from walking in our assigned purpose. Worst of all, it leaves us with a false impression of who God is and, more tragically, a scaled-down opinion of His mercy and grace.

Lewis B. Smedes, a professor at Fuller Theological Seminary, defines *shame* as: "A vague, undefined heaviness that presses on our spirit, dampens our gratitude for the goodness of life, and slackens the free flow of joy. Shame . . . seeps into and discolors all our other feelings, primarily about ourselves but about almost everyone and everything else in our life as well."[3] Psychologist and author John Bradshaw believes shame "is a healthy human feeling that can become true sickness of the soul" and describes toxic shame as spiritual bankruptcy and a "state of being, a core identity. Toxic shame gives you a sense of worthlessness, a sense of failing and falling short as a human being. Toxic shame is a rupture of the self with the self. It is like internal bleeding. . . . an inner torment."[4]

We don't like to talk about shame because it is messy. Like Adam and Eve, our instinct is to hide our shame. We attempt to cover it with modern-day fig leaves ranging from addictions to breakneck busyness. We bury our shame beneath perfectionism, good deeds, and yes, even ministry service. Been there, done that. Some people are more prone to experiencing feelings of shame, while others seem better equipped to avoid its sting with a healthy understanding of guilt and grace. Those who grew up in households where shame was a mainstay of the family diet will often turn around and serve it in their own families, passing it down from generation to generation.

Shame is not the same as guilt. Guilt says, "What you did was bad." Shame says, "What you did was bad; therefore, you are a bad person." Shame is not the same as regret. Regret says, "If I could go back and do things differently, I'd do this or that." Shame says, "I'll never get it right. I'm a failure." Shame is not the same as embarrassment. Embarrassment says, "Everyone experiences embarrassing moments." Shame says, "Yet another reminder that I'm a loser and nothing will change that fact." Guilt is always connected to *behavior* while shame is always connected to *identity*. While guilt draws us toward God, shame sends us away from God.

Shame on Me . . . Again

I was recently reminded of my propensity to lapse into shame mode when I tackled a master-closet makeover. I love clothes. I love shoes. If I'm sad, down, stressed, or just in need of an escape, I don't race to the nearest liquor store or watch endless hours of reality TV. I hop into my car and head to T.J. Maxx or Marshalls. I'm aware of the problem and, with God's help, am making slow and steady progress. Emphasis on the word *slow*.

My closet makeover was a reminder of my tendency to escape into fashion. One glance at the giant pile of clothes and shoes in the middle of my bedroom floor and I was awash with shame. Like Adam and Eve, I had no place to hide. My fig leaf was ripped away and my sin was exposed (though I must admit there were plenty of garments available to cover it up!). The shame tapes began to play in my head. *When will you get this problem under control? If your readers could see this display of waste and materialism, they'd never buy another book you write. Look at that skirt with the tags still on it! Think of the families who have only the clothes on their backs—your pile of discards could clothe them for a lifetime.* And on and on the mental beat down continued.

And then there are the flashbacks of my more grievous encounters with shame. These are much more difficult for me to talk about. Quite honestly, I'm still unpacking that lockbox in my soul. I can certainly see why so many people choose to numb their shameful memories with alcohol, drugs, food, and other unhealthy addictions. Anything to quell the hiss of shame that taunts us in our moments of weakness and despair. Despite our attempts to bury the shame under good acts or even bad vices, shame doesn't die when we bury it—we simply bury it alive. Ironically, the end result from attempting to bury our shame is yet more shame. Piles upon piles.

The Truth About Shame

God uses conviction to bring about sorrow and change, not shame. In one of his letters to the early church in Corinth, Paul wrote, "For godly grief produces a repentance that leads to salvation without regret, whereas worldly grief produces death" (2 Cor. 7:10). Shame hijacks God's nudges of conviction and turns them into a toxic landfill of self-loathing. Repentance is hard when your nostrils are filled with the stench of shame and you're convinced that stench has reached the heavens.

In Romans 7, Paul wrestled with guilt brought about by conviction:

> For I do not understand my own actions. For I do not do what I want, but I do the very thing I hate. Now if I do what I do not want, I agree with the law, that it is good. So now it is no longer I who do it, but sin that dwells within me. For I know that nothing good dwells in me, that is, in my flesh. For I have the desire to do what is right, but not the ability to carry it out. For I do not do the good I want, but the evil I do not want is what I keep on doing. Now if I do what I do not want, it is no longer I who do it, but sin that dwells within me. (vv. 15–20)

We've all been there. Guilt. Conviction. The pull toward sin. More guilt. More conviction. The desire to do good. The regret of caving in. Do you recognize the pattern? But then we see in the passage when Paul, like so many of us, faced a critical moment where his guilt stood at the crossroads of healthy conviction and toxic shame and he chose the wrong road: "Wretched man that I am! Who will deliver me from this body of death?" (Rom. 7:24).

In Paul's defense, he may have spoken out of a deep understanding of his sinfulness apart from God's grace. However, as a believer, Paul was a new person with a new identity. Post-grace, Paul was not a wretched man because his identity at that point was hidden in Christ. Post-grace, Paul did wretched things, but he himself was not a wretched person. He accurately summed up the misery that results when he asked, "Who will deliver me from this body of death?" Shame, left unaddressed, is a body of death. While the Greek word for *death* refers to "the physical death of the body," it can also mean "all the miseries arising from sin."[5] I've known this tug-of-war Paul spoke about and can vouch firsthand for the misery that permeates every corner of your soul when sin lapses beyond healthy conviction that leads to godly sorrow and develops into full-blown shame.

One particular sin in my past (when I was a believer and should have known better) left me so bogged down with shame that it produced an endless cycle of emotional self-flogging that went on for many years. I had convinced myself that I deserved to carry the shame for the remainder of my days as part of my punishment or penance to God. A counselor friend pointed me to the passage of Scripture above and particularly the answer to Paul's question, "Who will deliver me from this body of death?"

Romans 7:25 holds the key (and by key, I mean a literal key as well that unlocks the shackles of our shame and sets us free in grace): "Thanks be to God through Jesus Christ our Lord!" Jesus has carried our sin and our shame to the cross. To continue to carry the burden would minimize the power of the cross. Shame takes the spotlight off God's redemptive work and puts it on us. Christ alone has given us the ability to conquer shame and declare with confidence, "There is therefore now no condemnation for those who are in Christ Jesus" (Rom. 8:1). Shame condemns. The cross sets us free. *The Message* translation says it this way: "With the arrival of Jesus, the Messiah, that fateful dilemma is resolved. Those who enter into Christ's being-here-for-us no longer have to live under a continuous, low-lying black cloud." Have you been living under a continuous low-lying black cloud? The good news is that God provides the antidote. The sun is shining behind the clouds. Jesus has carried your shame to the cross.

Confronting Our Shame

Author and research professor Brené Brown has dedicated a decade to studying the impact of shame. In an interview with Oprah Winfrey, she noted, "Shame needs three things to grow: secrecy, silence, and judgment."[6] As a remedy she encouraged vulnerability as the key to conquering shame. In chapter 4 we discussed how the discipline of confessing our sins to each other can help reduce shame and put the past in its place (James 5:16). Confession is not a one-time event. It is a discipline for the believer. Our struggle with sin and shame is not just limited to our past. I'm a big proponent of having someone in your life (an accountability partner or trusted friend) to whom you can bare your soul without hesitation on a regular basis. I have two friends that I meet with on a fairly consistent basis with whom I can be completely open when it comes to struggles and temptations I am experiencing.

If shame grows in secrecy and silence, the logical remedy for destroying its power is to bring it out of the darkness and into the light. If we are to live wholehearted lives, we must be willing to confront our shame. I know this is a difficult thought for many of you. I'm certainly not suggesting that you give a detailed account of every sin or shameful event in your life to anyone who is willing to listen. A first step would be simply to acknowledge your struggle with shame to a trusted friend, or if necessary, a Christian counselor.

I think it's important to note that not all shame is the result of personal sin. My heart aches for those who, by no fault of their own, were left carrying a burden of shame as the result of someone else's sinful actions. Abuse, regardless of whether it's mental, physical, verbal, or emotional, can leave a trail of shame that can wreck a life if not addressed. I have personally felt the sting of this brand of shame and can attest to the heartache that can occur when it is left locked in a vault of silence and secrecy. It wasn't until I was willing to confront that shame with a trusted friend (who also happens to be a Christian and a counselor) that I realized the freedom I'd been missing. Regardless of whether our shame is the result of our own sin or the sins of others, the result is always the same: if left in the darkness of secrecy and silence, it will fester and grow. If brought into the light, it will die.

No doubt our fear of judgment plays a huge part in our decision to keep our shame tucked away under a cloak of secrecy and silence. While God responded beautifully to Adam and Eve's sin and sorrow by clothing their nakedness with garments He personally made for them (Gen. 3:21), the Christian community is not always as kind in its response. In fact, many people rip off the fig leaves and march the guilty parties through the center of the garden in a parade of shame.

Shame, the Verb

We often think of shame in terms of being a noun, but it can also be a verb. You can *feel* it or *deal* it. Or, if you're like me, both.

The definition of *shame* as an action verb is "to cause to feel shame; make ashamed; to cover with ignominy; or reproach; disgrace."[7] As I've taken a more honest look at my life, God has made me aware of my tendency not only to feel shame, but to deal shame. What is it about human nature that makes us so susceptible to staging public lynchings? Is it our need to see justice? Or perhaps a subconscious desire to feel better about our own depraved nature? When Ted Haggard, former pastor of a thriving megachurch and leader of the National Association of Evangelicals, was in the news in 2006 for hiring a male escort for sex, I'm ashamed to say that my go-to reaction was one of self-righteous anger and disgust. It's okay to mourn the public consequences that occur when unbelievers see yet another example of God's people misbehaving badly. But my reaction went beyond mourning and launched straight into the courtroom. I picked up my gavel and appointed myself as judge and jury. At the height of my judgment, I shared with others openly, "I don't know how his wife can stay with him." Father, forgive me.

Shortly after Ted Haggard's downfall, I watched a show in which he and his wife were interviewed. His remorse seemed sincere and genuine. His wife was a model of strength and dignity. They spoke of God's forgiveness and how their faith had become stronger in the aftermath. I was awash with shame (or I should say conviction!). Who was I to shame this man when I had my own list of depraved deeds that have managed to escape the spotlight?

I recently read an article in which the author confessed to a similar self-righteous and shaming attitude about the Ted Haggard scandal. He recounted a lunch he was having with an atheist friend. Upon seeing the Ted Haggard story on a TV set in the restaurant where they were dining, the friend pointed to it and said to the author, "That is the reason I will not become a Christian. Many of the things you say make sense, Mike, but that's what keeps me away."

The author responded, "Hey man, not all of us do things like that." He wrote in the article that his friend laughed and said, "Michael, you just proved my point. See, that guy said sorry a long time ago. Even his wife and kids stayed and forgave him, but all you Christians still seem to hate him. You guys can't forgive him and let him back into your good graces. Every time you talk to me about God, you explain that He will take me as I am. You say He forgives all my failures and will restore my hope, and as long as I stay outside the church, you say God wants to forgive me. But that guy failed while he was one of you, and most of you are still vicious to him." Then he uttered words that left me reeling: "You Christians eat your own. Always have. Always will."[8] I wept when I read his words because I've been the very Christian he speaks of. Ironically, as a former agnostic, there was a time when I echoed his opinion of Christians.

If this grace is so amazing, why are we so stingy when it comes to dispensing it to others?

Shamelessly Shameless

It's important that we don't ascribe shame to God. God never administers shame. On the contrary, where shame is present, the enemy is not far away. Satan, the accuser, loves nothing more than for a believer to live under a dark cloud of shame. Believers who choose to remain shackled to their shame are hardly an endorsement for God's grace. I imagine Satan smiles every time one of God's children chooses to engage in the shame game. I can't help but wonder the magnitude of the kingdom's impact should God's people refuse to play this game another day and boldly approach the throne of grace instead.

Hebrews 10:22 reminds believers to "draw near to God with a sincere heart in full assurance of faith, having our hearts sprinkled to cleanse us from a guilty conscience and having our bodies washed with pure water" (NIV). Do you have a guilty conscience? Draw near to God with a sincere heart in full assurance of faith. The Greek word for *full assurance* is *plērŏphŏria*, which means "entire confidence."[9] There is no room left for doubt. Our sin and shame have been nailed to the cross. To carry shame after receiving Christ's provision for it is to doubt the power of the cross.

Hebrews 4:16 commands us, "Let us then with confidence draw near to the throne of grace, that we may receive mercy and find grace to help in time of need." And while 1 John 3:18 is a reminder to love not in "word or talk," but in "deed and in truth," the verses that follow speak powerfully to the shame that tries to condemn us: "By this we shall know that we are of the truth and reassure our heart before him; for whenever our heart condemns us, God is greater than our heart, and he knows everything. Beloved, if our heart does not condemn us, we have confidence before God" (vv. 19–21). In verse 20, *condemns* means "to find fault with, blame; to accuse, condemn."[10]

Shame works overtime to blame and condemn us in our hearts. I find it interesting that this passage of Scripture speaks of specific actions we can take (obeying His commandments, abiding in Christ) that will "reassure our heart before him" and, in turn, give us "confidence before God." Shame is defeated when we respond to our sins with confession based in godly sorrow that leads to repentance. If we are believers and we continue in sin, we can expect that our hearts will be heavy with conviction. God never intended repentant sinners to carry a burden of shame. And God certainly never intended innocent bystanders to carry a burden of shame as a result of someone else's sin. Ever.

I recently read about a Texas judge who handed out an unusual sentence to a convicted drunk driver. The driver had killed a man while driving under the influence, and he was ordered to stand at the scene of the crash for the next four Saturdays from 9 a.m. to 5 p.m. while wearing a sign admitting to his guilt. The judge also required the defendant to keep a picture of the crash in his living room as part of the punishment, and probation officers would visit the crash site and conduct random home visits to ensure the orders were followed. Apparently, this was the man's second DUI, and the judge must have felt that his selfish and sinful choices would continue to put innocent others into harm's way unless the defendant felt the sting of shame. Some commended the judge for the sentence while others felt it was barbaric.[11]

I read about another case in which a Seattle-area criminal was ordered to walk around town wearing a T-shirt that read, "I am a convicted child molester."[12] In yet another case, Memphis judge Joe Brown (who now has his own TV show) once allowed the victims of a theft to take anything they wanted from the robber's home in full view of the neighbors.[13]

These judges' orders got me thinking. What if God (the ultimate Judge) employed a similar tactic with us and made us wear a sign every time we sinned? It's a cringe-worthy thought. "I just told a lie." "I gossip on average of five times a day." "I'm having an affair with a coworker." "I lied on my taxes." Some people might be caught off guard at some of the signs God would hand them—things they've minimized or played off as unimportant in comparison to others. "I spend more than I make and have accrued mounds of debt." "I am cold and uncaring to my spouse." "I would rather work late at the office than spend time with my family." "I say that my money belongs to God, but I refuse to share it with Him." "I have denied my spouse sex for over two months." "I spend more time each day interacting with virtual friends on social networking sites than I do with God."

I wonder if it would make us think twice before pointing to the sins of others if our own sins were exposed for all to see.

The Gospel Court

God doesn't require us to carry around signs advertising our sins and shortcomings. Jesus lugged our sins up Calvary's hill and nailed each one to the cross. If you carry a burden of shame, you need to revisit the cross. The Judge has spoken. The sentence has been handed down. The cross spoke over our hearts: "No longer condemned."

It brings to mind the story of the adulterous woman in John 8:3–11. You might remember the story. The Pharisees, in an attempt to trap Jesus, brought a woman caught in adultery to Him to ask His opinion about her punishment. They reminded Jesus of the law of Moses and the command to "stone such women." They asked Him, "So what do you say?" Jesus responded to their question by bending down and writing in the sand. The Pharisees, always persistent in their folly, asked their question again. Jesus stood and replied, "Let him who is without sin among you be the first to throw a stone at her," and He bent down again and resumed writing in the sand. His answer pierced their souls, and in that brief moment, their consciences were stirred. They walked away, but their retreat was rooted not in a newfound sense of compassion for the woman but, rather, in a fear of their own sins being exposed. Once gone, Jesus was alone with the woman.

I want you to stop for a moment and try to picture the scene. The crowd is gone, and Jesus and the woman are left alone. Jesus is bent over and writing while the woman stands before Him and waits for Him to speak. As Saint Augustine once said, "The two were left alone, *misera et misericordia*" ("a wretched woman and Mercy").[14] Every second must have seemed like an eternity to her as she waits for her sentence. And then Jesus stands and speaks: "Woman, where are they? Has no one condemned you?"

Perhaps the woman raises her eyes to His for the first time and replies, "No one, Lord." Ponder the irony of this next moment. He is the only one who met the conditions He had given to the crowd of accusers just moments before when He declared, "Let him who is without sin among you be the first to throw a stone at her." And then Mercy speaks, "Neither do I condemn you."

In the gospel court we, too, stand alone with Jesus, our sins exposed, wretched women and our judge, Mercy. I have been this wretched woman. Have you? I wonder how many of us have wasted precious days, months, and even years hiding our faces behind our hands in shame, waiting for a verdict that was handed down long ago. Jesus, both our Judge and Redeemer, has spoken, "Neither do I condemn you." Why then, do we condemn ourselves?

Are you burdened by unresolved shame? Go ahead. I dare you to come out of hiding and take a peek. Mercy is waiting to set you free. He's been there all along.

COMING CLEAN

1. Have you experienced a painful encounter with shame? Describe the circumstances. Have you ever shared the story with anyone? If not, prayerfully consider who might be a safe confidant to help you unburden this story.

2. What is your most recent encounter with shame? What were some of the messages or "shame tapes" that played in your head?

3. Adam and Eve responded to their shame with fig leaves. What fig leaves (or escapes) do you commonly use to cover up your shame?

4. Can you think of a time when a healthy dose of conviction over a sin led to godly sorrow, which, in turn, led to repentance? Did you allow the shame tapes to continue to play after you had repented?

5. How have you played a part in "dealing shame" to another person?

6. I love the beautiful picture we get in Genesis 3:21 when God responded to Adam and Eve's nakedness (and shame): "And the LORD God made for Adam and for his wife garments of skins and clothed them." How does this image speak to your heart regarding your own shame?

7. How did the story of the woman caught in adultery and, specifically, Jesus' response to her, minister to you?

Chapter 6

Law and Disorder

*I have always found that mercy bears
richer fruits than strict justice.*

—Abraham Lincoln

The Holiday House was a quaint, family-owned hamburger joint with a classic diner feel. It was located a few blocks down the road from the private school my children attended in their grammar school years. Sometimes I would meet fellow mom friends there for a late lunch before carpool duty beckoned. When family came into town for Grandparents' Day, we would often end the evening at the Holiday House with a round of desserts.

The restaurant was tucked away in a small shopping center in an established West Austin neighborhood called

Tarrytown. The center had been built in 1939 and had quite a bit of history attached to it. In the early years, it attracted visitors from all over who came to visit the state capitol, which is about ten miles away. The Holiday House had been in the shopping center for fifty years, along with several other businesses that had survived and thrived over the decades.

But all that changed in 1999, when upon her mother's death, the shopping center was inherited by the granddaughter of the original owner. If you lived in West Austin in the late nineties, you could not escape hearing the tale about Tarrytown and its villain, Jeanne Daniels, who was at the center of the story. Daniels was a radical animal rights activist, so she refused to renew the lease to the Holiday House restaurant because it served meat products. Other casualties included a family-owned Chevron gas station that had opened in 1941 and had run a successful business for sixty-seven years before running crosswise with Ms. Daniels. She schooled the gas station owner about candy bars he sold, which were "made from milk that was presumably ripped from the udders of helpless cows."

One by one, businesses closed or chose to relocate due to the stringent lease requirements that prohibited the sale of animal products or any item that might be deemed harmful to animals. And by "animals," let me clarify, this included the protection of ants, rats, and even fish eggs. Various tenants were given a list of contraband items: gift baskets containing jars of caviar were banned at a liquor store, mousetraps at a hardware store, leather eyeglass cases at an optometrist's office, and shoes and belts at a children's clothing store. When one shop owner complained about an infestation of ants and requested an exterminator for her shop's exterior, she was told that the pests would be trapped and "relocated."

Daniels's crusade on behalf of animals was carried out at the expense of the economic livelihoods of shop owners and their employees. A magazine article appearing in *Texas Monthly* referred to Jeanne Daniels as "the terror of Tarrytown."[1] At the end of the day, I doubt Ms. Daniels's long list of narrow-minded rules and regulations won over many converts to her cause. Like many, I am a huge animal lover, but the bullish tactics she employed to enforce compliance left me wanting to look up her address and eat a dozen hamburgers on her front lawn in protest.

Another Landlord Story

The year was 1987. I was a newlywed and a fairly new believer when my coworker walked in one morning and slammed her purse down on her desk while angrily declaring, "You Christian people piss me off." I really liked my coworker, and in many ways, she reminded me a lot of myself a few years prior—angry at Christians and cynical about organized religion. Having once been on the receiving end of Christians behaving badly, I could relate to her perspective. I had worked hard to get to know her before engaging her in any discussion about my newfound faith in Christ. I was just beginning to make some progress, and she had even asked a few questions about my faith. And now this.

"What happened?" I asked as she situated her things on her desk, making as much noise as possible to vent her anger. She finally sat down and turned her office chair toward me.

"I'll tell you what happened," she snapped. "My idiot land-lord stopped by a few days ago to check on an A/C repair in the duplex I rent from him. While he was there, my boyfriend walked out of the bedroom, and I politely introduced him to my landlord. You could tell by my landlord's expression that he seemed bothered, but I just chalked it up to his frustra-tion over the expensive A/C repair." She grabbed her purse and aggressively began to riffle through it, finally extract-ing a document. Waving it in the air, she continued, "So this morning I'm walking out the door on my way to work, and this letter was taped on my front door." She thrust the letter in my direction. "Go ahead. Read it."

I can't recall verbatim what the letter said, but it contained a sampling of Scripture verses about "fornication" and "sav-ing sex for marriage," all of which were preceded with "God's Word says" and were sourced at the end with the exact Scripture reference as a bonus. My eyes widened and I shook my head back and forth as I read. I told her, "I'm so sorry. God's Word also says a lot about loving people with the love of Christ, but your landlord must have skipped those verses."

She softened when she sensed my sincere sorrow for what had happened, so she unloaded further, "Did you see the last part? About how he doesn't feel comfortable renting to me, now that he knows that my boyfriend stays over on some nights? Or the part where he said I have until the end of the month to move out because renting to me would compromise his faith and values?"

I was floored. Speechless. And then came the anger. When I finally regained my composure, I reassured her that not all Christians behave this way. But the damage was clearly done. Any progress I had made toward introducing her to the mercy and grace of a loving God went down in flames with the landlord's letter.

But here's the part of the story that still haunts me to this day: in a desperate attempt to find reassurance that this Jesus I had placed my trust in was not the Jesus of the Christianity that was portrayed in the landlord's letter, I recall bringing the situation up to other believers. Some of their responses, which supported the landlord's actions, left me confused and dismayed.

So what is the difference between the animal rights landlord and the Christian landlord? Both held firm to their dogma and beliefs. Both laid out a rigid mandate that required that their tenants follow their personal convictions. Both refused to renew leases to tenants who wouldn't adhere to their rules. The only real difference was the object of their passions.

Here's a question to ask yourself: Did you find yourself nodding in disbelief at the first landlord's behavior, horrified at the lack of compassion displayed for the people on the receiving end of her relentless animal rights campaign? Let me ask you a more difficult question: Were you equally as horrified over the actions of the Christian landlord? Or did a tiny part of you feel somewhat conflicted over his plight, arguing that he was simply holding fast to his convictions, even if his presentation was somewhat less than perfect? But wait. Isn't that exactly what the animal rights landlord was doing? Holding fast to her convictions? I am certainly not suggesting that it's wrong to have personal convictions, but rather making the higher point that enforcing our personal convictions on others is rarely (if ever) an effective strategy to win converts to any belief or cause.

If you're not quite sure how you're feeling at this point, that's okay. This is heavy stuff. As Christians, we will face many situations that leave us conflicted over what action (if any) to take. That being said, I want to issue you a challenge: resist the urge to skip this chapter. No matter where you are in your faith journey, chances are you have played the part of the legalist at some point. Even if you don't think legalism is an issue for you to examine in your own life, consider this chapter as a cautionary tale of how easily Christians can pervert the gospel by hitching a laundry list of rules and regulations to God's grace.

The Purpose of the Law

Before we dive into the rampant problem of legalism, I think it's important to talk about the purpose of the law (that is, the Old Testament rules and regulations) for believers in the twenty-first century. The apostle Paul answered that question in Galatians 3:23–25:

> Before the way of faith in Christ was available to us, we were placed under guard by the law. We were kept in protective custody, so to speak, until the way of faith was revealed.
>
> Let me put it another way. The law was our guardian until Christ came; it protected us until we could be made right with God through faith. And now that the way of faith has come, we no longer need the law as our guardian. (NLT)

Other verses remind us that, because of the Savior, we are no longer "under the law." However, this does not mean we have permission to *ignore* the law. With Christ's death, we were set free from the *curse* of the law. Galatians 3:13 states, "Christ redeemed us from the curse of the Law, having become a curse for us" (NASB). This certainly does not free us to sin, knowing that the penalty of our sin has already been paid. However, Romans 6:1–2 speaks to the problem of this cheapened grace when it says, "What shall we say then? Are we to continue in sin so that grace may increase? May it never be! How shall we who died to sin still live in it?" (NASB). Later, in the same chapter, Paul added, "What then? Shall we sin because we are not under law but under grace? May it never be!" (v. 15 NASB).

The law and its rigid requirements serve to remind believers of their need for a Savior. We are not bound to that law because of grace. That grace should move us to a place of grateful obedience, not continued disobedience. The problem with legalism is that it takes the focus off of that grace and puts it back on the law. The word *legalism* does not appear in the Bible, but it is defined in the dictionary as "strict adherence, or the principle of strict adherence, to law or prescription, especially to the letter rather than the spirit."[2] Most of us will dip our toes into the tide of legalism from time to time, but too often our tendency is to see legalism as a fault in *others* while excusing it in our own lives. Many of us deny our own legalistic leanings. Often we miss God's nudges of conviction because we've convinced ourselves that those other Christians out there have the problem. We can even point out "those other Christians." Ironically, we're probably on *their* lists!

The Root of Legalism

The primary root of legalism is an improper understanding of God's grace. God's grace amounts to "Jesus + nothing," while legalism suggests "Jesus + some things." When I became a believer in 1987, I was drawn by the message of grace and the invitation to come just as I am. When I heard that there was no need to perform for God's love or approval, I could hardly believe it. Having been a lifelong performer and people pleaser, I truly felt as if I'd been set free. In those initial months I couldn't keep quiet about God's grace and frequently shared my faith with others from an overflow of gratitude for what Christ had done for me. Yet somewhere along the way being a believer became less about grace and more about following the rules. It wasn't a conscious shift in my theology of grace. I still held fast to a belief that grace was "Jesus + nothing." However, I began to develop strong opinions about how God's people *should* live in light of the grace they've been given. I created a standard for myself and others based on outward behavior.

I'm sure my shift toward legalism occurred in part because a good majority of the Christian teaching we hear today (some of my own included) focuses heavily on formulas for pleasing God (what we do) but speaks little about our identity in Christ (who we are). Most of us don't think we need a remedial tutorial on grace, but the truth is, many of us didn't really allow it to seep into our souls and become the foundation of our faith the first time around. It's hard to wrap our minds around the equation that "grace = Jesus + nothing" when we've been told our whole lives that "you can't get something for nothing" and "nothing in life is truly free."

When I think back on my early years as a believer, I sensed an unspoken agreement among God's people that you could speak openly of this grace and give it lip service, but practicing it might indicate that you lacked the necessary "fruit" to prove a true salvation experience. From the card-carrying legalist's perspective, dipping one toe in the tide of grace and freedom could lead to a foot in the water, then both feet, followed by wading out to waist-high water. Then, *zap*! Before you know it, you've been carried away by the undertow of licentious living. To avoid this slippery slide, your safest bet is to stay as far away from the water's edge as possible. As if the freedom part of grace was just an afterthought or merely a theological construct. What a miserable trap!

Admittedly, it's often hard for us to balance this idea of grace and freedom with clear warnings in Scripture that urge us to avoid the very appearance of evil (1 Thess. 5:22). Navigating the gray areas of faith is not an easy task for any believer. The legalist, however, takes it upon herself to dissect the gray matters and neatly file each one under a category of black-or-white, yes-or-no, do-or-don't. The goal of the legalist is to toe the line spiritually (according to her own list of rules and regulations) for the sake of *feeling* spiritual. A good day for the legalist amounts to a spiritual to-do list on which the good-deeds column is heavy with check marks and the sin column remains blank. Of course, it is impossible to go a day without sinning, and therein lies the trap. The daily MO of the legalist is to "stay right with God" by doing all the right things, ignoring the powerful truth of Galatians 5:1: "For freedom Christ has set us free; stand firm therefore, and do not submit again to a yoke of slavery."

The glorious truth is that Christ has released us from a lifelong prison sentence of being bound by the law. With His death on the cross, Jesus paid the penalty and opened the cell door. Legalists cannot bring themselves to leave the cell. Sadly, the longer a legalist stays in her cell, the more comfortable she begins to feel in her self-imposed restrictive environment and the less comfortable she feels about the world on the other side of the prison wall. It would be easy to feel sorry for legalists since they subject themselves to an impossible standard, but they aren't happy to remain in their cells alone. They live by the motto, "misery loves company," and this is certainly true for the legalist. They cannot tolerate the thought that other believers would dare to live in freedom, so they taunt, judge, coerce, and manipulate God's children to return to the prison yard.

Who, Me? A Legalist?

In my collection of vintage magazines, I recently stumbled upon a prime example of legalism in an article published in 1896. The author was in a tailspin over a new trend to use age-appropriate puzzles and other resources to help engage children in the Bible:

> There is a sin prevalent in our households of which we take little note, which, in fact, we encourage by an indifference to it, or an active participation in its folly and wickedness: the use of the Word of God for the purpose of making riddles, conundrums, puzzling questions, anagrams, etc., etc., out of it. . . . We need not be astonished if the boys and girls who have been permitted to turn the leaves of their Bibles for pastime and entertainment, turn them in after years to find pretexts for their infidelity. There has been, indeed, a singular laxity in regard to this sin; and that Divine Book which has been the comfort, the stay, the hope of humanity in all ages, has good reason in these latter days to make this mournful complaint: "I was wounded in the house of my friends."[3]

Oh my. Reading that makes me want to start a support group for all the poor Bibles (mine included) that have been forced to endure yellow highlighter pens and notes in the margins. I'm fairly certain the author of this article would have plenty to say about the children's leaflets found in many church bulletins on Sunday morning with seek-and-find word games highlighting key Bible verses. Or, heaven forbid, what about the heathen parents who allow their children to engage in weekly Bible drill meetings or Vacation Bible School? If you think that would be upsetting, the author probably would need smelling salts to recover from a glimpse of a typical Sunday morning in most any church where children, youth, and adults alike are pulling up Bible verses on their phones and tablets. Sheer wickedness, I tell you—their poor Bibles left behind on their nightstands crying out for attention! On the positive side, the pages are pristine and well preserved in obedience to the verse that says, "Thou shalt not have a well-worn Bible." Oh wait, that isn't a verse. Never mind.

While it seems ridiculous to us that someone would be so visibly upset by such a trivial issue as Bible puzzles, we have no shortage of legalists in our churches today who, in a similar fashion, expect believers to adhere to their own long lists of personal (not biblical) convictions. Legalists feel safer in a world where progress can be evaluated and measured. A world where there are distinct markers (even if they are self-imposed) to gauge their spirituality. Allow me to step on some toes (my own included) by presenting a few examples of legalistic attitudes common among many believers today.

Have you ever grumbled (either out loud or to yourself), "I don't understand how Christians/people who say they love God could _____."

- align themselves with the _____ political party
- not vote
- allow their children to participate in Halloween or believe in Santa
- shop at stores who say "Happy Holidays" instead of "Merry Christmas"
- send their children to public school
- drink alcohol
- get a tattoo or body piercing
- listen to secular music
- watch secular TV shows and movies
- attend the _____ concert
- miss church for their children's extracurricular sports
- use the _____ Bible translation
- not tithe (10 percent of income) to their local church
- not attend church regularly
- wear a bikini / two-piece / halter dress / shorts / miniskirt
- have a contemporary service or not sing hymns/not have Sunday school
- raise their hands during worship / not raise their hands during worship

- buy a lottery ticket
- drive a luxury car / spend that much on a house
- believe / not believe _____ (insert a minor theological doctrinal position here)

If that doesn't convict you, consider the following list, and ask yourself if any of these apply to you.

I feel as if I'm disappointing God if:
- I fail to say grace before a meal.
- I fail to have a regular and consistent quiet time.
- I don't share my faith on a regular basis.
- I don't confess my sins on a daily basis.
- I don't pray for my pastor / country / unsaved neighbor / elected officials / child's teacher / best friend's child who is a prodigal, and so on.
- I'm not involved in serving at my local church.
- I fail to attend the evangelism training program at my church.
- I'm spiritually unmotivated.
- I don't find a way to turn every conversation toward Jesus when talking with my coworker / the person sitting next to me on my flight / the door-to-door salesman / my child's teammate's mother who is sitting next to me, and so forth.

If you're still not sure if legalism is an issue for you, let me ask you this difficult question: What is your default, gut-level, go-to reaction when you see or hear of a fellow believer engaging in a liberty that you don't personally agree with? Is your first thought one of righteous indignation, or do you have an attitude of grace? Do you find yourself wondering how that believer could possibly have come to a different conclusion than you did? Or do you trust that the believer has the same access to the Holy Spirit that you do, and (a) may have been led in a different direction or (b) may be slower to respond to conviction? Maybe your legalistic expectations are directed not at others but, rather, at yourself. (I would argue that the two go hand in hand.) I want you to take a minute to search your heart and ask yourself this question: How do I feel when I don't measure up to my own spiritual expectations? (See the previous list for examples.)

Let me confess to you that I failed for the most part when asking myself the above questions. Though I've greatly improved in my own struggle with legalistic thinking, I have a terrible habit of thinking that my personal convictions should also be your personal convictions. I have also done plenty of time in the prison yard of self-imposed good deeds. I'm referring to the mental list of tasks performed for the sake of feeling more *spiritual*.

For example, there was a time in my life when if I missed a morning quiet time (reading my Bible), didn't pray a "hedge of protection around my children," didn't pray before a meal, and so forth, I felt shameful before the Lord. This eventually led to a woe-is-me attitude of "I never measure up, so why bother. I quit." When you imagine a God who shakes His head back and forth with disdain and an eye roll every time you fail to perform, you will respond in one of two ways: (1) You will clean up your act and dutifully perform out of fear of His disappointment or, even worse, His wrath; or (2) You will distance yourself from God because you don't feel comfortable in His presence.

Either way, you're still in the prison yard.

Let's imagine for a moment that someone has lapsed into the trap of toeing the line and being dutifully obedient out of a fear of disappointing God and incurring His wrath. This person performs out of a sense of duty, imagining that this is what is required to please God. Her passion and fire are long gone, but by golly, she has racked up a whole lot of check marks in the do-good column, so she reasons she must be on the right track.

Now let's imagine a believer who has failed to do all the right things for months upon months. And let's say she stumbles in a big way (think of the prodigal son). She feels a deep conviction over her sin, and as a result, she returns to God, desperate for His help. Grateful that Mercy met her in her mess, she opens her Bible, prays, and now sits in the same church as our other friend—the dutiful one. Which one has a more authentic and intimate relationship with God? I am certainly not suggesting that we need to take the path of the prodigal to experience a revival in our souls. My point is that God wants our obedience to be the result of a deep sense of *gratitude* for His grace and mercy, not the means of *attaining* His mercy. You don't have to go hog wild (sorry, couldn't resist the prodigal play on words) to experience this gratitude. It comes from an understanding of what it means to be set free from the law.

Set Free from the "Shoulds" and "Should Nots"

Years ago I hosted a houseguest who used my guest bathroom. She dutifully informed me upon her inspection that my toilet paper roll was not hung right. She was half-joking, but yeah, I can't be your friend if you're that rigid. My bathroom, my rules. And, for the record, there are no rules when it comes to my bathrooms, unless it pertains to the toilet seat not being raised by certain male creatures. My no-rules philosophy is also extended to the dishwasher. I bantered in a fun-natured debate with a family member years ago over whether or not the silverware should be loaded up or down in the dishwasher basket. Can we just agree that there is more than one way to load a dishwasher or hang a roll of toilet paper? If you're a legalist, you probably can't. In a similar fashion, legalists major in spiritual minors.

The attitudes of our hearts reveal more about our legalistic thinking than what we say we believe about God's grace. Some Christians are very public about their personal convictions (for example, posting smug comments about moral issues or political rants on Facebook, Twitter, blogs, etc.). Others are more passive-aggressive in their legalism, resorting instead to an eye roll, smirk, or patronizing head shake when they catch wind of a fellow believer who doesn't adhere to one of their personal convictions.

The apostle Paul knew the pull toward legalism would be so powerful for believers that he spent a great deal of time warning his readers about the dangers of legalistic thinking. The cautionary warning he issued to the believers at Colossae is a timely warning for legalists today:

> If with Christ you died to the elemental spirits of the world, why, as if you were still alive in the world, do you submit to regulations—"Do not handle, Do not taste, Do not touch" (referring to things that all perish as they are used)—according to human precepts and teachings? (Col. 2:20–22)

While I believe that most Christians will struggle with legalism on some level, I don't believe most legalists would qualify as full-fledged Pharisees, the elite legalists in the New Testament. Jesus saved some of His harshest words for the Pharisees. In one passage alone, He referred to the Pharisees as "hypocrites" seven times; He called them "blind guides" five times and "fools" twice. He even called them "serpents" and a "brood of vipers" (Matthew 23). Yikes.

Interestingly, the Greek word for *hypocrites* in this chapter is *hupŏkritēs*, which means "an actor, stage player; pretender."[4] It was a term used mostly for the theater to talk about the roles people would play and the masks they wore. Pharisees were religious pretenders who boldly rejected the gospel of grace and unashamedly insisted that true followers of Yahweh adhered to every letter of the Old Testament Law. Jesus summed up the Pharisees when He said, "These people honor me with their lips, but their hearts are far from me. They worship me in vain; their teachings are but rules taught by men" (Mark 7:6–7 NIV).

Believers may be guilty of behaving like the Pharisees at times, but for most folks sitting in our churches on Sunday mornings, their legalism is the result of a *misunderstanding* of God's grace rather than a *blatant rejection* of God's grace. A true modern-day Pharisee believes that salvation is gained by our own efforts and good deeds or a combination of works plus Christ's atonement for our sins. I don't think most believers fall into that narrow category of being modern-day Pharisees, and for that reason I've chosen to highlight the brand of legalism that is more commonly practiced among God's people today. A cure for this kind of legalism does exist, but it may take several rounds of treatment before we see improvement in our lives.

Purging Our Churches of Legalism

The longer I'm in ministry, the more collateral damage I see in churches and ministries where legalism has been allowed to remain unchecked among members. Show me a church that has divided or split at some point along the way, and I bet we can trace the root cause to a handful of grumblers with a leaning toward legalism and a list of grievances a mile long, such as:

- "The pastor doesn't use the _____ translation of the Bible when preaching."

- "The choir / worship team doesn't sing enough hymns."
- "There are too many announcements at the end of the service."
- "The church spends too much money / not enough money on _____."
- "The church doesn't have deacons / elders."
- "The sanctuary is too cold." (Okay, I'm busted on this one.)

There is nothing wrong with holding strong preferences when looking for a church to call home, but sometimes our piddly preferences can morph into a legalistic mind-set that is rooted in a belief that there is only one right formula for doing church—or for living the Christian life. There is no such thing as a perfect church because churches are composed of imperfect, sinful people. However, legalists have set high standards and rarely do those standards center on reaching the lost or becoming a safe place for flawed believers to gather and grow in the likeness of Christ.

Someone once said, "Things that matter most should never be at the mercy of things that matter least."[5] Let's not forget that our call as Christians is to make much of Jesus. The Great Commission calls us to make disciples of Jesus, not to recruit other people to a works-based lifestyle that makes *us* feel better (for a while) and makes *them* feel like constant failures. We are sharing the gospel, not hawking a product for commission. We must emphasize grace before we talk about commitment, because once grace becomes a believer's identity, commitment will follow. Timothy understood this truth when he wrote, "For the grace of God that brings salvation has appeared to all men. It teaches us to say 'No' to ungodliness and worldly passions, and to live self-controlled, upright and godly lives in this present age" (Titus 2:11–12 NIV). On the contrary, if you emphasize commitment to a checklist over the grace of God, the end result is almost always legalism.

I question why we as believers focus so much of our time and attention on teaching about the dangers associated with sin, but we turn a blind eye to the insidious dangers of legalism. I believe there is no bigger threat to our ministries and churches than legalism. Ask your friends who don't attend church (both Christians and non-Christians) why they stay away. Many of them will confess that Christianity or the church represents a long list of impossible rules to follow. When did our churches cease to be a safe place for wounded, imperfect people to gather and receive grace? The apostle Paul recognized the dangers of legalism and spent more time addressing it (with a defense of grace) than any other sin. He wrote Romans and Galatians to defend the gospel, but what was he defending it from? Legalism.

The only cure for legalism is to live a gospel-centered life. We must steep our souls in grace and keep it at the forefront of our hearts and minds. We must continually remind ourselves that, from beginning to end, God's love has pursued us, wooed us, and saved us. We must cling to the startling reality that we can do nothing to make God love us less, and we can do nothing to make God love us more. His love for us is perfect, relentless, and constant. Grace is the foundation of our faith—not a mere pillar or support beam.

Without grace, Christianity ceases to be different from any other works-based religion or cult. Christianity without grace is powerless. Every moment spent highlighting spiritual minutiae is a moment when grace is shoved out of the spotlight and into a corner. Jesus + nothing = grace. Nothing could be more scandalous. And nothing could be more true.

In the light of that truth, we can take off the shackles of dos and don'ts, shoulds and should nots, us and them, and walk in the glorious freedom of a relationship steeped in grace. We can walk out of the shadows of our own faulty self-sufficiency and soak in the warmth of Mercy's light. We don't have to live another day in our prison cells of legalism. Nor do we have to join those who choose to stay.

COMING CLEAN

1. What was your initial reaction upon reading the story about the animal rights landlord? Upon reading the story about the Christian landlord? If you were in the Christian landlord's shoes, how might you have handled the situation?

2. On a scale of 1 to 10, with 10 being extreme, where do you rank in regard to being legalistic? Is this an area where you have felt God's conviction?

3. When it comes to the shoulds and should nots, in what ways are you guilty of believing others should abide by your self-imposed rules?

4. Is legalism a problem in your church? If so, describe how you might play a part in being a positive influence for change.

5. If you lean toward legalistic thinking, what are some factors that hinder you from emphasizing grace?

Chapter 7

Get More "Likes"!

*He who seeks for applause only from without
has all his happiness in another's keeping.*

—OLIVER GOLDSMITH

I stared at my computer screen for upwards of four hours today before typing the title you just read. I chalked it up to writer's block initially, but here's the truth: I don't want to write this chapter. This is strange, because when I originally outlined the chapters for this book, it was one of the chapters I was most excited to write. But that was when I was experiencing a brave moment and thought it would be cathartic to come clean about my own desperate need for approval. Now I feel as if I've been in a wrestling match all day with God. Here is a summary of the tug-of-war that has been raging in my soul:

GOD: Tell them the truth. They can handle it. Many people reading this will be able to relate.*

ME: But, God, how about I share some other people's stories and how they search for approval in all the wrong places? I could fill a whole chapter with Facebook status messages that are nothing more than desperate cries for an esteem-boosting "like."

GOD: Would you be including some of your own in that list? (He snickers playfully.) Because you've been guilty of baiting for "likes" a time or two or twelve, no?

ME: Ouch. Okay, how about this? What if we compromise and I share some of my personal struggles with wanting approval but subscribe them to someone else? You know, change the names to protect the guilty?

GOD: Vicki, the main theme of this chapter is to care less about what others think and more about what I think. And I think you have nothing to lose by being honest. How can you encourage your readers to "come clean" in this area of their lives if you aren't willing to take the same step?

---

* Disclaimer: Please note that God did not speak to me audibly. I am not a mystic, nor do I believe any kind of New Age hoopla. And yes, my need for approval has probably led me to include this disclaimer and go overboard in clarifying this point.

The bottom line is this: I'm embarrassed about how much your approval means to me. There, I said it.

I know the truth—I know that I am supposed to perform for an audience of One. I've said that in speaking engagements and written it in books. But my eyes are often on the wrong audience. Take, for example, this book. God's desire is that the content be pleasing to Him and bring glory to His name. But the truth is, I desperately want to write things that are poignant or funny and leave you wanting to call your best friend and read parts out loud until she begs you to stop.

When I write, I often have to ask myself, *Am I writing with the goal of impressing you, the reader? Or am I writing to please God because I am nothing more than a steward of the message He has assigned me?* If the book is written with the motive of pleasing God and it only sells a handful of copies, it is far more successful than if it is written with the motive of pleasing thousands and it lands on the *New York Times* bestseller list. My heart's desire is to write something that makes God smile and nod His head in approval. However, my fleshly desire for approval often hijacks my spiritual zeal.

I'm comforted by the fact that the apostle Paul, perhaps one of the godliest Christians to ever walk this earth, could relate to this tug-of-war between the flesh and the Spirit.

For am I now seeking the approval of man, or of God? Or am I trying to please man? If I were still trying to please man, I would not be a servant of Christ. (Gal. 1:10)

Galatians 1:10 is one of those verses we like to hurry past because if we camp on it too long, it might interrupt our lives. Many of us have been performing for the world's applause for so long that it has become our primary language. Seeking approval is as second nature to us as breathing. Every so often, we may get a gentle nudge from God that something is not quite right in our souls. In those moments when we recognize the nudge, we might even find ourselves asking, *Why do I do this?*

Have you ever felt any of the following nudges?

Why do I name-drop in order to impress someone I've just met?

Why do I gravitate toward name-brand clothes? Is it really because they're better made, or is it because I want to impress others?

Why do I engage in gossip, even though I know it's wrong?

Why do I hesitate to speak up when I disagree with someone about a gray area of Scripture that someone else is declaring as black-and-white?

Why does it bother me when one of my friends has more Facebook / Twitter / Instagram friends / followers / likes / comments than I do?

Why do I say yes to too much and pack the calendar full with so many activities—and then complain to everyone about how busy I am?

Why is it hard for me to say no to a ministry opportunity that would cause my family to get the short end of the stick?

Why do I sometimes dress for the opposite sex?

Why do I dwell too much on comments from critics?
Why is it so important to me that my children succeed / make
   the A team / win awards / make good grades?

Let me give you some possible reasons (in no particular
order):

- We want to be liked.
- We want to fit in.
- We want to be noticed.
- We want to impress people.

Or to sum it up: we are people pleasers. It feels *good* to get
a pat on the back. A smile and an affirming nod. A compli-
ment. A flirty wink. A fist bump. A hug. A Facebook "like."
A smiley face emoticon at the end of a text. A retweet. A
mention. A praise. An occasional catcall from a construction
worker. Those "atta-girls" are tangible and real. The applause
of others is intoxicating. It gives us a buzz that always leaves us
wanting more. We'd be lying if we said we didn't like approval
from others. There is nothing wrong with enjoying approval
from others, but it's unhealthy when it lapses beyond *I enjoy this*
to *I need this.*

Losing Yourself in Others' Opinions

Here's the problem with *needing* approval versus *enjoying*
approval: those of us who need approval become a slave to

the opinions and preferences of others, and we begin to conform to those preferences. Proverbs 29:25 says, "The fear of man lays a snare," and what a snare it is! The Hebrew word for snare is *môqêsh* (mo-kashé), which means "a noose (for catching animals) or a hook (for the nose)."[1] When we perform for the approval of others, we lose sight of who we really are—the person God intended us to be. We become an insincere version of ourselves. When that happens, it's only a matter of time before we begin to feel like frauds. And should the approval we seek ever diminish—or worse, disappear altogether—we don't know how to survive without it. It has completely ensnared us and has captured us like a noose around our necks. Should we try to move freely in any direction, we're choked by the need to be valued by others.

Paul reminds us that our primary aim or ambition is to be pleasing to Him: "Therefore we also have as our ambition, whether at home or absent, to be pleasing to Him" (2 Cor. 5:9 NASB). Chances are, we're all guilty (on some level) of esteeming others' approval above God's. If you're like me, you may set out with the intent of pleasing God, but somewhere along the way, you get off track. Before long, you've taken your eyes off God and you're focused on the crowd. Yet as good as others' approval can feel, it's always fleeting. If we're not performing for the sole goal of bringing glory to God, no amount of applause, pats on the back, Facebook friends, or Twitter followers will quell the silent ache in our souls for something more. I have felt this ache more recently than I care to admit. Sadly, many of us will attempt to soothe

the ache by looking for yet another buzz of approval. And so the addiction continues.

The Never-Ending Tryout

I've been a people pleaser for as long as I can remember. Some of us grow up in homes where approval is in short supply, and so, by default, we will look for it in other places. We desperately want to know that we matter, and the approval of others reaffirms that we have value and worth. But it's a catch-22. If outside approval determines our worth, then we become dependent on others to determine if we matter. We put our happiness in the hands of others.

I was in a furniture consignment store recently and inquired about a couple of chairs I was considering purchasing for my living room, but I wasn't quite sure they would match my current décor. When I approached a salesclerk and asked about the return policy, she informed me that I had the option of checking the chairs out on twenty-four-hour approval. In other words, I can take them home and give them a test-drive in my living room. I have the power to vote thumbs-up or thumbs-down. When we depend on the approval of others to determine our worth, in a sense we are trying out for the approval of others on a daily basis.

A need for approval can manifest itself in different ways. For example, one manifestation in my life was an inability to say no. I have been guilty of packing my calendar with so many activities, obligations, and ministry opportunities that should one of the activities not deliver the approval buzz I was subconsciously seeking, then plenty of other backups waited in the wings. In doing so, I safeguarded myself from an approval addict's biggest fear: rejection. As long as I could feel, touch, see, or experience approval in some tangible form or fashion, it must mean I'm okay. I matter. At least, in that moment. In essence, I was throwing a thousand darts up against a wall, hoping one or more would stick. The more darts I had in my pouch, the more likely I was to hit the approval target at some point. But even when I did hit the target, the buzz was always fleeting. It was never enough. I was always in pursuit of the next approval buzz.

Just Smile and Nod

In addition to always feeling like we are engaged in a never-ending tryout, people pleasing can cause us to lose our voices. I was struck by a passage in Scripture in the gospel of John:

> Nevertheless, many even of the authorities believed in him, but for fear of the Pharisees they did not confess it, so that they would not be put out of the synagogue; for they loved the glory that comes from man more than the glory that comes from God. (12:42–43)

Remember, God desires truth in our inmost parts, and that requires an honest appraisal of our existing patterns of behavior.

Have you ever been a part of a discussion among fellow believers and someone said something you didn't necessarily agree with, but you nodded your head and affirmed what was being said? When we feign approval of something for the sake of winning (or keeping) the favor of others, we have, in essence, lost our voice. Why do we do this? The answer can be found in verse 42: "But for *fear of the Pharisees* they did not confess it, so that they would not be put out of the synagogue" (emphasis mine).

Show me a people pleaser, and I'll show you someone who has a deep fear of rejection. That woman (or man) would rather lose her voice—forfeit the right to speak up and say what she really believes—and conform to attitudes and beliefs that misrepresent her than risk being "put out" of favor with _____. A people pleaser doesn't want to risk being put out of favor with her posse of girlfriends, her Christian book club gathering, her Sunday school class, the group of fellow volleyball moms—you fill in the blank. Yet the twisted irony is that in order to gain (or keep) favor, it is not the real you and the real me that is being accepted—it is merely a façade.

I can't help but wonder how many of us have fallen into Christian Stepford-like behaviors based on an insatiable need for approval. Think about it. When was the last time you challenged an opinion with a statement like:

- "I'm not so sure I agree with that. I think . . ."
- "I used to think that, but lately I've had the conviction that . . ."

- "Can we change the subject? I'm getting a little uncomfortable."
- "I don't really feel that way."
- "I disagree."

The truth is that, for many of us, using our voices to express dissenting opinion is tantamount to going before a firing squad. Maybe it's time we quit this people-pleasing charade and get our voices back (assuming we ever had a voice in the first place). I can't promise you that your polite resistance will be met with approval, but I can promise you that statements like the ones above will help you reclaim your voice and stay true to the person God is calling you to be. Wouldn't you rather be accepted for the person you really are than escape into a silent shell of yourself? Because what happens when you lose your voice permanently? Now there's a scary thought.

Ranking #32,587

I have a confession. In the process of writing this chapter, I fell off the I-won't-worry-about-the-opinions-of-others wagon. During a writing break, I hopped over to Amazon to see how my newest book release was doing in the rankings. (The lower the ranking number, the better; the better the sales, the higher likelihood you approve of the book. More important, that means you might like me.) I sighed audibly when the ranking wasn't what I'd hoped it would be. Gloominess set in. I logged on to Twitter and did a brief scan of the feed and saw an announcement in which several of my speaker friends were speaking at an upcoming women's event—and I wasn't included in the lineup. More gloominess. Pity party now in full swing. I headed to the pantry and grabbed my go-to comfort food. Cheez-Its in hand, I headed back to my laptop.

I'm a glutton for punishment, so I hopped on over to my Facebook author page, and (I kid you not) I was greeted with a solicitation from Facebook to "boost my status updates" in order to "get more likes" on my page. Out of curiosity I clicked the ad to see what it was all about. Apparently, you can pay a sum of money to turbocharge your status updates. Five bucks will rocket-launch your status updates to the top of the newsfeed of your current "likers" in the hopes that they will "like" what you said and in turn, their "like" will show up on their friends' newsfeeds, and *voila!* Their friends won't be able to resist the urge to hop over to your page and "like" you too. That's how it's supposed to work—in theory. Facebook gives you the option of paying as much as $300 to boost a post. I suppose for that sum, Facebook not only rocket-launches it to the top of selected newsfeeds, but sends their in-house enforcer over to your friends' houses to pay them a personal visit with vague threats to rough them up a bit if they don't click "like." Or something to that effect. You can hardly be mad at Facebook. They've simply tapped into our deep need for approval and figured out how to make big bucks on our insecurities. I had to laugh at the rather ironic timing of the promotion to get more likes while in the midst of my own personal pity party.

More Than a Number

If you have served in ministry in any capacity, chances are you've heard about the importance of expanding your platform, ministering to your tribe, or developing a brand around your organization. In the process of talking with several publishers about this manuscript, my agent and I had a conference call with one publisher who spent more time inquiring about my Twitter followers, Facebook friends, and "specific steps I was currently taking to increase my platform" than the actual message of the book. Sure, I understand that even in Christian publishing there is a risk involved, and publishers dance a fine line between being a ministry and paying the bills, but is this really what it has come to? I'm sure that publisher loved my candid disclosure that I sometimes go weeks without logging on to some of those social media sites and I'm currently taking no specific steps to "increase my platform."

With a standard like that in place, Jesus would have been turned away. During His three-year public ministry, He lost followers at a quicker rate than He gained them, so it's safe to say building His platform was not at the top of His list. It wasn't even *on* His list. Can you picture Him in a meeting with a potential publisher saying, "Oh, you want a platform? Just last week I spoke to over five thousand folks on a hillside. If only I'd had a book to hold up at the beginning of my session! Can you imagine the sales?! I think someone recorded my sermon, though, so we can offer it as a free promo for signing up for my weekly blog." My encounter with that publisher was an isolated experience, and the rest of the publishers I spoke with were more interested in the message God had given to me.

Everyone Gets a Vote

We live in the age of information. In less than five seconds you can find out information on just about everything imaginable. With that comes the ease of liking, ranking, following, and reviewing just about every product, service, business, or person on the Internet. Don't like the frozen waffle you ate this morning? With a few clicks on your smartphone, you can post a negative online review in less time than it'll take you to cut it up and put it in the dog's bowl. Not a fan of Oprah's new network? The president's State of the Union speech? Your neighbor's dog that barks incessantly? The bitter aftertaste of stevia in your morning coffee? (I hear ya on that one!) Blast it on Facebook. Trash it on Twitter. Review it on your blog. Everyone and everything is fair game. Nothing is off-limits.

Even businesses and product manufacturers are desperate to win the approval of others. They will turn cartwheels to get a *like* or a *follow* and will bribe you with ten dollars off your next order, free shipping, or whatever it takes to get consumers to push the magic Like button. Likes and follows have become the new gold standard for word-of-mouth marketing. Never mind if you didn't really care for the product or service. Which reminds me . . . did I mention that I will send you a free set of steak knives if you'll hop on over to Facebook and like me? Oh, I kid.

On the one hand, technology has given us a vote and a voice when it comes to the products and services we use. I love that I can pull up product reviews on my phone while standing in the aisle debating a purchase. I especially love that I have a voice when it comes to the new energy-saving clothes dryer I recently bought that has become the bane of my existence. Is it really energy-saving if the fancy sensor control shuts the dryer off automatically without your permission and leaves your clothes damp and unwearable? Is it really energy-saving if you have to run your dryer two or three times to get one load of laundry dry? No, it's not—and I've grouched about that fact on Amazon and given this lemon of a dryer a nail-in-the-coffin-one-star-but-I-would-give-it-less-if-I-could customer review. And let me tell you, it felt good to have a voice and a vote.

On the other hand, this digital age often causes us to give too much weight to the opinions of others. While I'm certainly healthier than I used to be when it comes to seeking others' approval, I'm fairly certain I would not have survived adolescence if Facebook, Instagram, Twitter, Vine, and the whole gamut of other social networking sites had been around in my day. I would have been the girl losing sleep at night wondering why her best friend got twice as many likes on the same photo they both posted earlier that day on Instagram. Or why my boyfriend posted a flirty comment on another girl's picture and followed it with one of those charming little winky-face emoticons. And let's not even begin to talk about the fallout that might occur if someone unfriended or unfollowed me. Several counseling sessions would be in order. And several boxes of Cheez-Its.

Recently I was visiting with a family friend's daughter who is in college, and we were discussing the pressure our teens must feel in a culture where "likes" have become the gold standard for gauging popularity. She shared that she was babysitting for a family when one of the girls (who is in middle school) started looking at her (the college girl's) Instagram pictures on her phone. She said the teen girl pointed to one picture and said, "You didn't get very many 'likes' on this picture. You should delete it so no one will see it. That's what I do when I don't get very many 'likes.'" Wow! How sad that this young lady has based her worth on the number of likes she can garner on a picture from people she will scarcely remember in ten years.

That story brings to mind a funny comic I saw recently. It showed a couple of people sitting in a room among row after row of empty chairs. At the front of the room was a coffin draped with flowers. A woman standing at the entrance is seen quietly whispering to a gentleman standing next to her, "He had over 2,000 Facebook friends. I was expecting a bigger turnout." It's intended to be humorous, but it certainly speaks to the futility of basing our worth on a virtual popularity vote of friends or "likers."

God Doesn't "Like"—He Loves

At the end of the day, there's only one like that really matters. In fact, like doesn't even do it justice. "But God shows his love for us in that while we were still sinners"—and extremely *unlikable*—"Christ died for us" (Rom. 5:8). The Greek word for *still* is *ĕti*, which means "now, still, after that."[2] Right now, even in the midst of our unlikability, His love does not waver. He sees down into the core of our souls (aka, our inmost beings). He knows us better than we care to know ourselves. And He loves us anyway. Layer after messy layer after messy layer, He loves us. And with this knowledge of God's love—in spite of our messy selves—comes a desire to put aside our people-pleasing ways and instead seek to please Him.

Because we are deeply, passionately, unequivocally, and unconditionally adored by the Lover of our souls, we can stop the approval-seeking, gotta-have-more-likes madness. Admit to the problem and take action. We can choose to live an honest, wholehearted life from this point forward, one day at a time. To fess up and take steps in the right direction.

I won't promise you it will be easy. I have experienced more anguish during the writing of this chapter than any other. Until I began to outline it and to dig deeper into God's Word, I didn't realize how deep my own people-pleasing tendencies ran. I have trudged through this chapter and vacillated back and forth between bravery (coming clean) and cowardice (relapsing back into the familiar). Yet I'm determined to live a transparent, authentic life from this point forward. If God delights in truth in my inmost being (Ps. 51:6), then I want to be brave and remove my people-pleasing mask to expose the problem—a problem that we can begin to deal with only when we begin to live in the confidence of the Father's love for us instead of others' approval.

COMING CLEAN

1. Think through your average day and take a quick inventory of some of your behaviors that could be labeled as "people pleasing" (or look over the questions on pages 124–25 if you need some help). Write down any examples that come to mind.

2. On a scale of 1 to 10, with 10 being "very important," how important is it for you to have others' approval? Why do you think that is?

3. Share a recent situation in which you did not receive the approval you had hoped for and it had a direct impact on your emotions or mood.

4. Can you think of a time when you went along with an expressed opinion, even though you disagreed, in order to conform and not make waves (that is, you "lost your voice")?

5. What sort of pressures (if any) do you feel when it comes to finding approval in the world of social networking?

Chapter 8

Buzz-Hopping

*A person will worship something, have no doubt about
that. We may think our tribute is paid in secret in
the dark recesses of our hearts, but it will out. That
which dominates our imaginations and our thoughts
will determine our lives, and our character.*

—RALPH WALDO EMERSON

I was driving through a small rural town one afternoon on
my way to do a little antiquing when I noticed an outdoor
market in the town square. (In the South *antiquing* is a legiti-
mate action verb, by the way.) My eye was particularly drawn
to a cluster of clothing racks containing a colorful assortment
of apparel items. I have a trained eye for fashion bargains and
this looked promising. Intrigued, I pulled over.

As I approached the racks, my heart began to beat faster. Was that the designer blouse I had lusted for from a high-end store but couldn't stomach the high-end price? There it was in all its glory—in my size and at a fraction of the cost! Did I mention it still had the tags on it? In fact, many of the clothes on the racks were brand-new or, at most, gently used. Strangely, they only came in one size—which just so happened to be my size! Pinch me. I began plucking item after item from the racks until my arm was aching from the weight of the clothes.

As if that wasn't enough, I discovered several bins of pricey designer jeans too. Some of the jeans still had the tags hanging from them and touted prices upward of $200. There was a beautiful red slash through the price and in its place, a handwritten price of $25. *What in the world is going on here?* I wondered. About that time a chirpy young sales assistant appeared at my side. "Ah, you look like you might be among the lucky few who can wear this size. Today is your lucky day." She offered to take the load of clothes off my aching arm, and I gladly took her up on the offer.

"So, yeah, what's up with the clothes only being one size?" I asked as I continued riffling through the designer jean bin.

The sales assistant went on to explain that the clothes belonged to the heir of a wealthy Texas rancher and "she was running out of room in her closet and decided to do a little spring-cleaning." I'm not making this story up. By the looks of the sale, I can only assume her closet must have exceeded the square footage of my home. I had just concluded that a nice clothing boutique was going out of business and the clothes were being offered in a sidewalk fire sale of sorts. I stood up from the jeans bin and turned to face the salesclerk.

"Do you mean to tell me that all these clothes belong to one woman and she hauled them over here from her personal closet?"

"Well, no, not exactly," the clerk replied. "She hired me to clean out her closet and haul the clothes over here and run the sale for her."

Of course she did, I thought to myself.

As the clerk walked away, I felt sick to my stomach. I was nauseated at the display of flaunted waste and excessive materialism. I am not exaggerating when I say this one woman's discard pile could have clothed an entire village. It was almost too much to bear. Hearing the actual circumstances behind the sale was a buzzkill. I ended up purchasing one blouse and passed on the other bargains. To buy anything more would have felt like buying drinks for an alcoholic at happy hour. I had never met the woman, but I most certainly met her idol that day on the town square.

Yes, I judged this woman. I crafted imaginary conversations in my head when, if given the opportunity, I would gently challenge this wasteful spender to donate her discard pile to a battered women's center and to work a day (or a month) in a soup kitchen. She needed fixing, and I was happy to step in and help her. And that's when it hit me. *Why do I so easily default to a holier-than-thou attitude when confronted with someone else's messiness?* Rather than judge this woman, I could pray for her. I know the emptiness that comes from chasing after false gods. The only difference between the heir to the wealthy Texas rancher and me is that my idols were safely tucked away and far from being exposed in the town square of judgment.

Exposing Our American Idols

Every one of us chases after idols. Many of us associate the word *idol* with the Old Testament wooden statues or the more popular golden calf. We read about the Israelites' fickle faith as they wavered back and forth between loving God and chasing after foreign gods of other nations, and we shake our heads in disbelief. *How could those stupid Israelites not see that those idols were worthless?* we ask ourselves. But are we really any different?

The truth is, we chase after our own modern-day gods. Our golden calves can be found in closets full of name-brand clothes or parked in three-car garages. Golden calves can line the shelves of our trophy cases or take the form of our followers on a social networking site. Many mothers fashion their own golden calves out of their children's accomplishments and successes. Golden calves can take the shape of food, drugs, the number of digits on a paycheck, or the digits on the scale. When we become more enamored with the *created* rather than the *Creator*, we are at risk of creating our own golden calves.

In his book *Counterfeit Gods*, author Timothy Keller asks

the question, "What is an idol?" He goes on to answer the question by saying,

> It is anything more important to you than God, anything that absorbs your heart and imagination more than God, anything you seek to give you what only God can give. . . . An idol is whatever you look at and say, in your heart of hearts, "If I have that, then I'll feel my life has meaning, then I'll know I have value, then I'll feel significant and secure."[1]

This is not to say we can't enjoy healthy pursuits and pleasures. However, when a pursuit or pleasure becomes the object of worship rather than a means for enjoyment, it becomes an idol.

Idols can almost always be traced back to what began as a mismanaged, mishandled lust or craving. Yet, much like a dish we may crave at a favorite restaurant, the satisfaction we experience in giving ourselves to a god is always short-lived. We may feel full in the immediate aftermath, but the craving will always return. It's only a matter of time before we're craving another buzz. It will never be enough to fully satisfy our hungry souls. This is not by accident. God has wired our hearts to seek satisfaction and fulfillment—in Him alone. C. S. Lewis once said, "I remind myself that all these toys were never intended to possess my heart, that my true good is in another world, and my only real treasure is Christ."[2] Anything else with which we seek to satisfy our souls will only be a false substitute.

Until we confront those idols, their power over us causes damaging consequences, even though we may be completely unaware. In his book *The Mortification of Sin*, theologian John Owen says,

> When a lust has remained a long time in the heart, corrupting, festering, and poisoning, it brings the soul into a woeful condition. . . . Such a lust will make a deep imprint on the soul. It will make its company a habit in your affections. It will grow so familiar in your mind and conscience that they are not disturbed at its presence as some strange thing. It will so take advantage in such a state that it will often exert itself without you even taking notice of it at all. Unless a serious course and extraordinary course is taken, a person in this state has no grounds to expect that his latter ends shall be peace.[3]

Idols stunt spiritual growth and leave us in a perpetual state of stuck. When it comes to our primary affection (what we in church call *worship*), we must choose God or the idol. God will *not* share the spotlight. It's not by accident that the first of the Ten Commandments is "You shall have no other gods before me" (Ex. 20:3). God is a jealous God and will not settle for first runner-up. The Old Testament is full of warnings and consequences of shoving God into the shadows in favor of the god of the month.

The book of Judges says the Israelites "would not listen to their judges but prostituted themselves to other gods and worshiped them" (2:17 NIV). In fact, the whole book of Hosea chronicles God's appeal to the nation of Israel to stop its adulterous relationship with idols and to turn back to Him (Hosea 2, for example). The language of these scriptures reveals how God feels about idolatry—it is an act of adulterous prostitution. It breaks His heart. Why? Not only because of His intense love for us but also because of the damage that can result when we pursue our idols. His tender heart toward us winces with the thought of what those consequences can do to us.

Dethroning the Idols

I recently took the bold step of broaching the topic of idols while my husband and I were out for dinner one night. We had an open and frank discussion about the idols that bid for our affection and threaten to dethrone Christ as our primary affection. I admitted that one of my biggest idol struggles was a tendency to put my children at the center of my life before they left the nest. My motive at the time was love, but my relationship with God often took a backseat when it came to my devotion to my children. My husband admitted that control and a need for security are the idols that he struggles with most often. By acknowledging the specific idols we struggle with, we exposed them to the light and kept them from thriving in secret.

If you don't feel comfortable discussing this topic with your spouse, I encourage you to find someone you trust who will be honest and hold you accountable (with a measure of grace and encouragement, of course). Author Brennan Manning notes,

> Honesty requires the truthfulness to admit the attachment and addictions that control our attention, dominate our consciousness, and function as false gods. I can be addicted to vodka or to being nice, to marijuana or being loved, to cocaine or being right, to gambling or relationships, to golf or gossiping. When we give anything more priority than we give to God we commit idolatry.[4]

If we are to move on in our faith, we *must* examine our hearts and souls for the presence of idols. Don't doubt that you struggle with idols. Everyone does. On this side of heaven, the enemy will do everything he can do to put *anything else* at the center of your heart. If you're not sure what you idolize, ask someone near and dear to you what idols are present in your life. If she knows you well, she will probably be able to tell you pretty quickly. Make sure you choose someone who will be honest and objective. I realize this is a radical step—or as John Owen said, an "extraordinary course."

If you still aren't quite sure what idols have captured your heart, try asking yourself the following questions:

- What preoccupies my time?
- What defines my worth?
- What are most of my daydreams about?
- What do I think about most when I'm in the car alone?

- What do I talk about most?
- What do I spend the bulk of my spare money on?
- What hobby or items take up the most space in my house?

It will be impossible to move on toward spiritual maturity until we identify and confront the idols that bid for our attention and affection. Some idols have such control over our lives that professional Christian counseling may be necessary. I have personally benefited from counseling over the years and have found it a safe place to discuss idols that have stolen my affection for God. Do whatever it takes to reorder or, if necessary, remove the idols that have captured your heart and become your primary affection.

Reordering Our Affections

Several months ago my husband and I decided to engage in a massive remodeling project in our home. Our kids have flown the nest, and with two off the payroll, we have some extra time and income to update our home. We agreed on a budget and hired a contractor, and I began creating my dream-house wish list on my Pinterest page. At first I enjoyed surfing the Web, looking at the never-ending list of possibilities. And when I say never-ending, I literally mean *never-ending*. Something as simple as choosing a kitchen cabinet door style could turn into mind-numbing hours of evaluating options. And that's only one part of the process. You have to choose the color of paint or finish, along with the cabinet knobs and drawer pulls. Brushed satin. Oil-rubbed bronze. Antique bronze. And that's just the cabinets. *Calgon, take me away.*

And don't even get me started on wall paint colors. Finding the perfect shade of tan for one room just about sent me to an early grave. A perfectionist should never be allowed to remodel a home. Ever. I was better off with the old system in which the builder gives you no more than three options for each step along the way and charges you a penalty fee if you change your mind. My breaking point came when I found myself staring at about half a dozen tan paint samples on my wall and suffering from what I like to refer to as "paralysis of analysis." After far too many minutes of debating with myself over one shade that had too much gray and another shade that had too much yellow, I snapped. *Who really cares which shade of tan I choose? Me, only me.* And that's the problem. In the timeline of eternity, the color of our walls doesn't matter. We will not have to stand before God and justify why we chose Oxford Tan over Mushroom Bisque on our living room walls, but we will have to account for the unhealthy amount of time and affection we devoted to the task. My conviction came when I realized I had poured more time into improving my house than nourishing my soul. Ouch.

I am certainly not saying it is wrong to enjoy certain pleasures—within reason. The danger comes when our enjoyment lapses into worship. Maybe for you it's an obsession over finding the perfect preschool for your little one. Or reaching a certain number on a scale. Or that hobby. Or the praise of others. The pull is different for each of us. My area of weakness may not necessarily be yours. If you devote too much time and energy to a pleasure that leaves you with little to no God-margin, an idol has taken up residence in your heart. Nothing—and I mean *nothing*—is a healthy substitute for your personal relationship with God.

Once we come clean about the idol chase and expose our idols of choice, we must reorder our affections. God comes first. Period. Even before husband and even before children. Other things fall into place. And we must learn to recognize the temptations and triggers that have lured us away from the Father in the past. Recovering alcoholics need to stay out of bars. If you struggle with buying things that are out of your price range, take a break from shopping. If you are easily rattled over salacious news stories that warn of economic disaster, stay off the online news sites. Or take a break from technology altogether. If you constantly think about the number on the scale, get rid of the scale. Recognizing your idols is an important first step, but unless you take steps to guard against them, they will continue to master your life.

When evaluating your idols, it's important to distinguish between pursuits that are *permissible* and pursuits that are *forbidden*. Some idols will need to be reordered, while others will need to be eliminated altogether. Let me explain. If you struggle with putting your children at the center of your life, that affection needs to be *reordered*. You might need to reduce the number of activities on the calendar or resist the urge to micromanage the details of their lives. You demote your children as the object of your primary affection so you can return Christ to the number-one spot. However, if your idol has become a sinful pursuit—an addiction, an affair, an illegal activity—you need to *eliminate* it altogether. A choice must be made: devotion to Christ or devotion to a sinful idol. Christ cannot sit on the throne of our hearts in His rightful place when we serve Him with double-minded devotion.

In the parable of the prodigal son found in Luke 15, the younger son faced a similar choice: he could leave his father and pursue his idols of pleasure, or he could remain in fellowship with his father. He chose to indulge his idols, and in doing so, turned his back on his father. He couldn't have it both ways. At his request, his father gave him his inheritance in advance. While the passage does not detail the exact timeline of events, verse 13 says the son "squandered his property in reckless living." We can only wonder what idols were represented in that one phrase—"reckless living."

Coming Home

The prodigal son spent his entire fortune to feed the idols of his life. Dying of hunger, he found a job feeding a farmer's pigs. I'm sure he had plenty of time to ponder his "before and after story" in the pigpen as he tossed the pigs their slop while his own stomach grumbled from hunger. Perhaps he even replayed the highlights of his revelry in the quiet moments, wondering where it all went wrong. He had chosen to worship his idols, and they had betrayed him. Idols have a way of doing that.

The hunger for satisfaction that drove the prodigal to chase idols was replaced with a different kind of hunger—the hunger for food. There, looking at the pigs he was hired to feed, he longed to eat the very slop he was feeding them. And in that critical moment, he finally came to the end of himself and his idols. Empty and joyless, he decided to return to his father and beg for a job. He never imagined such painful betrayal could ever be forgiven, but what happens next should offer hope to any believer who has ever turned away from God to chase idols:

> But while he was still a long way off, his father saw him and felt compassion, and ran and embraced him and kissed him. And the son said to him, "Father, I have sinned against heaven and before you. I am no longer worthy to be called your son." But the father said to his servants, "Bring quickly the best robe, and put it on him, and put a ring on his hand, and shoes on his feet. And bring the fattened calf and kill it, and let us eat and celebrate. For this my son was dead, and is alive again; he was lost, and is found." And they began to celebrate. (Luke 15:20–24)

It just doesn't make sense.

It's hard for me to recount the story of the prodigal son because I've been him. The story is oh so familiar. I know firsthand what it's like to pursue the idols of sinful pleasure and feel their temporary buzz of satisfaction. Like the prodigal son, I was eventually betrayed by my idols, and I found myself in the same pigpen, bogged down with the muddy mess of shame. Trust me when I say it's possible to attend church every Sunday, serve in ministry, and yet be far from God. While my wandering may have been unknown to others at the time, God knew it intimately. He watched me leave, but like a faithful Shepherd, He followed close behind. When I finally came to the end of myself, I looked up and there He was. Mercy was waiting in the distance to take me home. Rather than wag His finger in my face and scold me for my fickle faith, He embraced me with the same loving tenderness this father had for his child.

Hebrews 4:16 instructs us to "draw near to the throne of grace" with *confidence*, "that we may receive *mercy* and find grace to help in time of need" (emphasis mine). Many of us have read the account of the prodigal son and cast ourselves into the part of the younger son, but we see ourselves in the pigpen rather than the Father's sweet embrace. Perhaps you are stuck in the proverbial pigpen, lacking confidence to draw near to the throne of grace. You're content to just take on the task of a hired hand—going to church, performing your spiritual chores, but never approaching God in raw surrender.

Here's the deal: you won't be able to move out of the pigpen until you decide to look up. Start moving toward Him (and away from your shame), and you'll discover that He's already running toward you. Throw yourself into the embrace of grace and forgiveness. Until you've landed in the Father's arms and have attended the celebration party to follow, you will miss the impact of mercy. You can't be wrapped in Mercy's arms and hold tight to your idols at the same time. Idols can't compete with God's mercy.

Until Christ returns and we no longer wrestle with sin, we will always face the temptation to fashion idols and forget the impact of God's mercy and grace. In her book *A Confident Heart*, author and speaker Renee Swope wrote, "Until God's love is enough, nothing else will be."[5] We will continue to hop from idol to idol in search of satisfaction until we decide God's love is more than enough.

Mercy has spoken, and it's time to come home. Do you see Him in the distance?

COMING CLEAN

1. Can you think of a time when someone else's idol was exposed and you expressed a holier-than-thou attitude of disgust? What was the situation?
2. Reread Timothy Keller's definition of an idol on page 143. As you read the description, did God make you aware of one or more idols that may be present in your life? What did God reveal?
3. Have you ever openly acknowledged your struggle with an idol with someone else? If so, did it help you to bring it out into the open? If not, would you consider doing so for the sake of moving on?

4. What permissible affections have become the focus of your life and need to be reordered?

5. What forbidden pursuits have become the focus of your life and need to be eliminated completely?

6. What are some tangible steps you can take to guard against idols that threaten to become the object of your primary affection?

7. In what ways can you relate to the prodigal son? Have you experienced a time when you sought satisfaction in an idol and God met you in your mess and led you back home? Describe the experience.

Chapter 9

Prone to Wander

Not all those who wander are lost.

—J. R. R. TOLKIEN, *The Fellowship of the Ring*

"Mama, I messed up."

My college-aged son leaned in across the booth at our favorite breakfast spot as he whispered the confession. I held my breath, having already endured the "Mom, Casey's pregnant" announcement from his older brother, wondering if I was about to hear it again.

"I went to this party over the weekend, and I thought I could resist the temptation, but I gave in and drank." By the time he spit out the final part of his confession, I had already mentally drafted an announcement for my blog declaring I would never write another parenting book again. So you can imagine my relief when he confessed that his mess-up was drinking alcohol at a party over the weekend. I tried to resist jumping up, hugging his neck, and screaming, "Is that all, son?!" After, of course, I smashed in the glass case that contained a defibrillator on a nearby wall and gave my heart a quick jump start.

My son loves Jesus, and he knows right from wrong. He attends church weekly; he is a Young Life leader at a local high school and is involved in a weekly Bible study. He reads his Bible, and he prays. And he still messed up because that's what Christians do: they mess up. A lot.

A part of me was envious at the ease with which my son had made his confession. Those three words—"I messed up"—are hard enough to say to God, much less anyone else. What impressed me the most about my son's confession was that he had absolutely no interest in playing the pretender game. Not even with his mother. He strayed from God's path, recognized the error of his ways, and responded to the conviction with a godly sorrow that leads to repentance. My son did not doubt God's grace. He knew he was forgiven, and he was ready to move on.

On my drive home from the breakfast, I prayed for my son and thanked God for his tender heart that readily responded to the Holy Spirit's conviction. I thanked God that my son and I have the kind of relationship where he feels comfortable telling me about times when he stumbles or strays. And I thanked God for His grace that covers my son's sin—as well as my own. In the week that followed, I continued to think about the freedom that comes in being able to say those three words: "I messed up." Why is it so hard to admit to the tug-of-war we experience with sin on a daily basis? What if God's people could come clean about the struggle? What if we could be honest—not just with God, but also with each other?

The Pull

Putting our faith in Christ doesn't exempt us from sin. We will feel a constant pull toward temptation until we breathe our last breath. Why, then, are we so uncomfortable acknowledging the struggle? Paul certainly wasn't. In Romans 7:18–19 he admits, "For I have the desire to do what is right, but not the ability to carry it out. For I do not do the good I want, but the evil I do not want is what I keep on doing." I love Paul's honesty. When was the last time you heard a similar gut-level confession by a believer? Better yet, when was the last time *you* made a similar confession? I don't know about you, but I usually breathe a huge sigh of relief when a fellow believer musters up the courage to bring her struggle with sin out of hiding. Author Donald Miller recently tweeted, "I respect people who teach the truths of the Bible more when they also tell me the truth about themselves."[1]

True courage comes from telling the whole story of our lives—not just the highlights. When my youngest son went "off" to college (in the same town where we live), he started attending a church closer to campus. One of the things that sold him on the church was the humility he saw expressed by the pastor. My son shared how one Sunday the pastor confessed he had struggled with porn after he was married. I can't help but think this pastor's honest confession helped embolden my son to be honest about his own struggle with sin and come clean on the morning we met for breakfast with his own confession, "I messed up."

One of the things that drew me to Christ in my college years was the understanding that sin was a universal problem and that Christ was the only solution. Somehow I found comfort in knowing we're all in this together. We have all sinned. We *all* fall short of the glory of God. Not just some of us. All. Of. Us. Yet when I became a new believer, it was as if there was an unwritten rule stating that believers aren't supposed to openly admit to their ongoing struggle with sin. It felt like spiritual whiplash to hear "we *can* and *should* admit we are prone to sin," yet no one seemed to be willing to take the lead in admitting it. Every now and then you might hear a believer utter a vague reference to temptation, cloaked in popular Christian buzz phrases like, "There, but for the grace of God, go I," or my personal favorite, "Without Christ, I am capable of falling into any given sin on any given day." When I hear someone say that, I always want to reply, "Even *with* Christ, you are capable of falling into any given sin on any given day!"

Rarely do you hear honest conversation about the believer's battle with sin. Fearing the potential fallout, we have been conditioned to hide sin underground, away from others' wagging tongues and judgmental stares. Many of us can recall situations in which someone tried to be honest about his or her sin and received a quick dose of judgment from fellow believers rather than help or support. Or, heaven forbid, they learn that their private confessions have been shared with others, cloaked in the form of church-friendly prayer requests.

Believers are adept at engaging in diversionary tactics to avoid confronting their own struggles with sin. Some knock themselves out performing good deeds in an attempt to make up for their sins and faults. The logic goes something like this: "If my good deeds outweigh my bad deeds (my sins), I must be on the right track." Others try to divert attention away from their own sins by pointing a finger at others. Many believers readily turn the spotlight on the sins of others in an attempt to keep it far away from their own long lists. Evangelist Dwight L. Moody once said, "I have had more trouble with myself than with any other man."[2] You know you are maturing in the faith when you pay more attention to your own sins and faults rather than the sins and faults of others.

Another tactic believers use to divert attention away from their own sin is to engage in image maintenance rather than heart examination. Looking good is the name of the game for many Christians. As long as you can convince others you have your act together, you just might be able to convince yourself. Sadly, I have engaged in every one of these diversionary tactics at some point in my Christian journey. Only when I began to come clean and openly acknowledge my struggle with sin did I begin to move on and mature in my faith—because you can't fix what you aren't willing to admit is broken.

In his book *Abba's Child*, author Brennan Manning offers this profound wisdom: "Accepting the reality of our sinfulness means accepting our authentic self. Judas could not face his shadow; Peter could. The latter befriended the impostor within; the former raged against him."[3] The struggle with sin is normal. Pretending like the struggle doesn't exist is painfully unhealthy and stifles spiritual growth and maturity. We won't be able to move on until, as Manning beautifully puts it, we face our shadow and befriend the impostor within.

Mistaken Identity

It's the kind of news story that leaves you shaking your head in confusion. On December 17, 2012, the body of Timothy Henry Gray, age sixty, was found under the overpass of Union Pacific Railroad in Evanston, Wyoming. According to a coroner's report, the police found no signs of foul play and determined the cause of death was hypothermia.

But Gray wasn't your average transient. He was the adopted great-grandson of former US senator William Andrews Clark and the half-great-nephew of the reclusive New York copper heiress Huguette Clark, who had died the year before at the age of 104 with an amassed $300 million fortune. Gray was among twenty great-nieces and great-nephews who each stood to inherit $19 million from their great-aunt's estate. Attorneys for the relatives had been searching for Gray in the weeks before his death. Not that the fortune would have likely made much difference. Family members had not seen Gray in over two decades, claiming he had "severe post-traumatic stress symptoms due to childhood traumas." A coroner reported that at the time of his death, a wallet was found on him, and it contained undeposited checks from a few years back, one of which was described as "large."[4]

Timothy Gray's story is a desperately sad account of mistaken identity. Gray was an adopted heir who never realized his true worth. Instead, he chose to live as a homeless transient. You might be surprised to find we share something in common with Gray. We, too, are adopted heirs (Rom. 8:17; Eph. 1:5), as Paul told the church at Galatia:

> But when the fullness of time had come, God sent forth his Son, born of woman, born under the law, to redeem those who were under the law, so that we might receive adoption as sons. And because you are sons, God has sent the Spirit of his Son into our hearts, crying, "Abba! Father!" So you are no longer a slave, but a son, and if a son, then an heir through God. (Gal. 4:4–7)

Allow the truth of these verses to sink below your intellect down into the core of your being. You. Me. Adopted. By the God of the universe. Free to call Him *Daddy*. In spite of this life-altering truth, many believers suffer from their own cases of mistaken identity, failing to ever accept their true worth and standing before God. No longer are we alienated from God. We've been adopted by the One who owns "the cattle on a thousand hills" (Ps. 50:10). Sadly, many of us will go to our graves as spiritual paupers, sitting on fortunes of unspent blessings and benefits from God's great storehouse of grace.

Take, for example, the mistaken identity many believers ascribe to themselves when they say they are a "sinner saved by grace." For the majority of my years as a believer, I have readily identified myself as a sinner saved by grace. While it is true that I will continue to struggle with sin until I meet Jesus face-to-face, the truth is that sin no longer defines me. In fact, Scripture calls me (and you) a saint. Part of the reality of our 2 Corinthians 5:17 transformation (old things have passed away, new things have come) is the new identity we assumed on the day we became believers. Our old sinner-selves were crucified with Christ's death on the cross. Paul said it this way:

> I have been crucified with Christ. It is no longer I who live, but Christ who lives in me. And the life I now live in the flesh I live by faith in the Son of God, who loved me and gave himself for me. (Gal. 2:20)

Thanks to the finished work of Jesus Christ, we are sanctified and given a new identity as saints. Paul called believers "those sanctified in Christ Jesus, called to be saints together with all those who in every place call upon the name of our Lord Jesus Christ" (1 Cor. 1:2).

You may think I am being nitpicky over simple semantics when I state we are not just sinners saved by grace. To say we are sinners saved by grace is like saying we are indentured servants who owe God, rather than adopted children who are free to serve Him out of love. If we fail to recognize our true identity, we will forfeit the power God has bestowed upon us in the transformation process from sinner to saint. If we define ourselves primarily as sinners, that title can act as a self-fulfilling prophecy. Author Steve McVey says,

If you believe you are fundamentally a sinner, your default setting will be to act like a sinner. To behave in any other way would be to act inconsistently with the person you perceive yourself to be. After all, what do you expect a "sinner" to do? Sin. Sinning is simply the normal behavior for a sinner.[5]

I remember a particular moment when the reality of who I am in Christ began to set me free. Until that moment I had seen myself as "a sinner saved by grace." When I sinned, I would remind myself of God's grace, but my focus was on stopping the sinful behavior. Because it is our nature to sin, I felt like I was caught in a never-ending battle when I would sin yet again. I was trying to live as a saved sinner—which contradicts my core identity. I was simply living up to my own low expectations. Even if I could overcome one area of sin, another temptation was always waiting in the wings to trip me up. It was exhausting. It certainly didn't feel like the victorious life I had read about in the Bible, and I felt anything but free.

Perhaps, saddest of all, this brand of Christianity began to feel like nothing more than a regimen of behavior in which the end goal was perfection. After all, that's what sinless behavior produces, right? My walk as a Christian had been reduced to a sin-management program, not a growing relationship with the One who set me free. I looked for just the right formula of spiritual disciplines, rules, accountability, and anything I could find to combat the sinner within.

As a disclaimer, I am not suggesting these things won't help thwart sinful actions. My point is simply this: alone, apart from the power of Christ and apart from our true identity as saints, spiritual disciplines just won't do the trick. Charles Spurgeon once said, "I have found, in my own spiritual life, that the more rules I lay down for myself, the more sins I commit."[6] In Colossians 2:20–23, Paul warned of relying solely on self-imposed regulations, saying that "they are of no value in stopping the indulgence of the flesh" (v. 23). No matter how hard we try, rules and regulations won't kill our sinful appetites because rules feed our flesh. Without God's power, rules are futile at stopping sin.

For me, the transforming moment came when I found myself standing at a crossroads of a temptation—again. I had stumbled in that area before, and I was on the verge of taking the same wrong path—again. I couldn't muster enough strength to keep me from choosing the wrong path. I needed help. The Holy Spirit whispered a simple yet profound truth into my heart: *This is not who you are.* The reality of what Christ had done flooded my heart. Just as Paul had said, "I have been crucified with Christ" (Gal. 2:20). I, too, could say the same. Old, pre-saved sinner Vicki had been crucified, and in her place was a new creation. When Christ was resurrected, with Him came my new post-Christian identity.

I was transformed from a sinner to a saint. His goal in saving me was not just to forgive my sins, but also to leave me with the power to be alive in Him—a resurrection power to overcome sin.

In *The Practice of the Presence of God*, Brother Lawrence wrote,

> I consider myself as the most wretched of men, full of sores and corruption, and who has committed all sorts of crimes against his King; touched with a sensible regret, I confess to [Him] all my wickedness, I ask His forgiveness, I abandon myself in His hands that He may do what he pleases with me. The King, full of mercy and goodness, very far from chastising me, embraces me with love, makes me eat at His table, serves me with His own hands, gives me the key of His treasures; He converses and delights Himself with me incessantly, in a thousand and a thousand ways, and treats me in all aspects as His favorite.[7]

Do you see yourself in a similar light? My turning point came when I was overwhelmed by a deep understanding of what Christ had done. Filled with goodness and mercy, He met me in my mess and reminded me of my true identity as a saint. As a result, I wanted to live up to my new identity— one I didn't deserve but had been given with God's gift of mercy and grace. Christ had overcome the grave, and with that same power, I, too, could overcome sin and temptation and live a victorious life. I was set free!

Oh sure, I still stumble and fall from time to time, but I get up and remind myself, *This is not who I am.* Saints are not chained to their sin. Saints have the power to overcome sin. Saints walk in freedom. I'm a saint, and, therefore, I want to behave like a saint, not a sinner.

What is your identity? A sinner saved by grace, or a saint who still sins? Mercy has declared you a saint and is waiting to set you free.

On Our Way

A few days before I was scheduled to fly out for a speaking engagement, I received an urgent request from the pastor's wife of the church hosting the event. She wanted me to contact her immediately. I automatically assumed it was a church conflict or an unexpected tragedy and, as the weekend speaker, I wanted to make sure I was sensitive to the situation. I dialed her number and wasn't the least bit prepared for the news that followed.

Ashley was soft-spoken but perfunctory in her tone, almost as if she feared she might lose her courage if she didn't hurry up and tell me the reason for her original call. "I wanted you to be aware of a situation that has rocked our church family. I discovered last week that my husband, the senior pastor, is having an affair with a staff wife."

I was stunned. To add even more heaviness to her heartache, she went on to share how the staff wife and her husband were close friends of Ashley and her husband. It was almost too much to process as I listened to her bombshell news. I marveled that she was even able to make the phone call, much less tell the story before the dust had even settled. If I had been in her shoes, I'm fairly certain I would be curled up in a fetal position and rocking back and forth in a dark corner. After, of course, I had thrown my husband's belongings out onto the front lawn and had the locks changed. Oh, I kid. But not really.

I offered words of empathy to her fresh pain, knowing it would do little to soothe the deep wound, and I assured her that I completely understood if she needed to cancel the event. But Ashley insisted that the event take place as previously planned. She felt it was God's perfect timing and thought it would minister to the women of the church as they processed their own shock. I supported whatever decision she made and admired her ability to put the needs of the women in her church above her own.

When I arrived at the event, I had the privilege of spending some time with Ashley. I cannot begin to tell you about the deep courage this sweet woman of God demonstrated in the aftermath of the travesty. Wait, did I say *aftermath*? Correction: *she was still in it.* She spoke of her pain, but also of her confident assurance that God was at work behind the scenes to bring good from the situation. Mind you, this woman's world had been turned topsy-turvy just days before. One day her husband was the pastor of a fast-growing church, and the next day he was stepping down to be replaced with an interim pastor. With the discovery of the affair, she lost the security of her marriage, her husband's job, her own financial security, the loss of what she thought had been a true friendship with the other couple, and the ongoing fellowship of her church family. And, on top of all that, she had to worry about the security of her own children and how to navigate some difficult conversations with them. It was a mess.

In spite of all she was juggling on her emotional plate, the event was amazing. God showed up in full force, and Ashley closed out the event by stepping onto the stage and expressing her unwavering trust in God to restore her marriage, her life, and her future. But she also said something so profound that I doubt I'll ever forget it. Through her tears, she shared how she had told God that if He needed to shake up her security and her circumstances to do a greater work in her husband's life, it would be worth it. In other words, she told God, "Bring it."

I've stayed in touch with Ashley, and my husband and I recently had the privilege of meeting her and her husband for dinner. She had contacted me to let me know they were in my hometown to participate in a round of intensive marriage counseling. In fact, it was Ashley and her husband who gave me the beautiful wooden lap desk I described in chapter 4. As I mentioned, Ashley's husband responded in the aftermath of the affair with a deep sorrow over his sin. He was eager to see restoration in his marriage, his ministry, and most important, his relationship with God.

Only sincere, godly sorrow will lead us to true repentance. Author Jerry Bridges wrote,

God's Grace is greater than all our sins. Repentance is one of the Christian's highest privileges. A repentant Christian focuses on God's mercy and God's grace. Any moment in our lives when we bask in God's mercy and grace is our highest moment. Higher than when we feel smug in our decent performance and cannot think of anything we need to confess. . . . That is potentially a glorious moment. For we could at that moment accept God's abundant Mercy and Grace and go forth with nothing to boast of except Christ Himself, or else we struggle with our shame, focusing on that as well as our track record. We fail because we have shifted our attention from Grace and Mercy. One who draws on God's Mercy and Grace is quick to repent, but also slow to sin.[8]

Remember Ashley's declaration at the end of the event? God answered that prayer. Rather than spending years buried in bitterness and shame (or, for that matter, choosing to continue in sin), Ashley's husband met Mercy in the mess and took Him up on His offer of restoration. Ironically, Ashley emerged with a greater sense of security (in her God, rather than in her circumstances). Today their marriage is strong, and God has taken their faith to a new depth. Ashley and her husband have been able to move on because they turned to God in the midst of their mess. In fact, they both look forward to sharing their testimony of God's unmatchable love and mercy wherever He may lead them to serve in the future.

The Path of Repentance

When confronted with our sin, the first step toward healing begins with a sincere confession of sin. If you need proof that God is far more concerned with the condition of your heart than your list of transgressions, look no further than the story of King David. This same man—referred to as a "man after [God's] own heart" (1 Sam. 13:14)—gave in to his wandering, lustful eyes and started down a path that led him into adultery and murder (2 Sam. 11). Yet, amazingly, God still chose to have Jesus' lineage run through David's line. What a picture of grace! David declared:

> *Oh, what joy for those*
>   *whose disobedience is forgiven,*
>   *whose sin is put out of sight!*
> *Yes, what joy for those*
>   *whose record the LORD has cleared of guilt,*
>   *whose lives are lived in complete honesty!*
> *When I refused to confess my sin,*
>   *my body wasted away,*
>   *and I groaned all day long.*
> *Day and night your hand of discipline was heavy on me.*
>   *My strength evaporated like water in the summer heat.*
>
> *Finally, I confessed all my sins to you*
>   *and stopped trying to hide my guilt.*
> *I said to myself, "I will confess my rebellion to the LORD."*
>   *And you forgave me! All my guilt is gone. (Ps. 32:1–5 NLT)*

You and I will stray from God's path from time to time. Some wander in the open landscape of their faith while others drift in the hidden garden shed of their soul. Some people are more proficient in hiding their sin struggles than others. The problem is that we get caught up in classifying sin (big or small) and associate walking away from God with the *big sins* that land on the front page of a newspaper. I bet if we could tally up the number of believers who have left our churches over the years to openly pursue the world's pleasures, we'd be surprised to find just as many sinners sitting in our churches on Sunday morning, privately turning away from God.

If you are straying away from the Father (remember the story of the prodigal son in Luke 15), whether publicly or privately, I want to encourage you to do something: think of a fellow believer whom you trust and come clean with her. Ask her to get together and tell her about your struggle. Make sure you choose someone who will lovingly remind you of your identity in Christ (translation: "This is not who you are!"), commit to pray for you, and check in with you on a regular basis. Sin and shame lose power when shared in the light.

One of my favorite hymns is "Come Thou Fount of Every Blessing." It was written by Robert Robinson, who lived in the 1700s. When Robinson was a small boy, his father died. Without the guidance and influence of a father, Robinson eventually fell into the wrong crowd and became very rebellious. His turning point came when he and several friends went to heckle the great preacher George Whitefield. But instead Robinson walked away converted after hearing Whitefield's preaching. He became a minister and wrote the powerful lyrics to "Come Thou Fount of Every Blessing" that we sing in so many churches today. There is one part of the hymn that effectively describes the pull of sin that is common to believers of every generation:

> *Prone to wander, Lord, I feel it,*
> *Prone to leave the God I love*
> *Take my heart, O take and seal it*
> *Seal it for thy courts above.*[9]

Robinson was no stranger to the pull of sin. In fact, a widely told story indicates that he eventually fell away from the faith. The story goes that one day, while riding in a stagecoach, he overheard a female passenger with an open hymnbook in her lap, humming his particular hymn. He asked the woman what she thought of the hymn and he began to cry. He told the woman, "Madam, I am the poor unhappy man who wrote that hymn many years ago, and I would give a thousand worlds, if I had them, to enjoy the feelings I had then."[10]

We *all* are prone to wander from our faith. In Revelation 2:4–5, Jesus spoke about the danger of forgetting our first love: "But I have this against you, that you have abandoned the love you had at first. Remember therefore from where you have fallen; repent, and do the works you did at first."

"Remember therefore from where you have fallen." We must make it a regular discipline to reflect on the times we have fallen, and more important, recall the mercy that met us in our past messes, put us back on our feet, and led us back to God's path. Remembering how God has rescued us in the past will help us avoid those wrong paths again in the future. Remembering also puts God's grace on the forefront of our minds, instead of on the back burner, where it often sits unnoticed. C. S. Lewis once said, "We all want progress, but if you're on the wrong road, progress means doing an about-turn and walking back to the right road; in that case, the man who turns back soonest is the most progressive."[11]

It is impossible to move on unless we experience a godly sorrow over our sin that leads to repentance. Have you strayed from God's path? Is there a sin that hinders you from moving on and becoming the person God created you to be? It's never too late to turn back to the right road. Mercy is waiting to show you the way.

COMING CLEAN

1. When was the last time you made a confession that sounded a lot like, "I messed up"? Do you have someone with whom you are comfortable sharing your struggle?

2. Have you practiced any of the diversionary tactics noted on page 159 to hide your struggle with sin?

3. When it comes to your core identity, do you see yourself as a sinner saved by grace or a saint who

still sins? If you are struggling to see yourself as
a saint, what is your hesitation?

4. When was the last time you recall experiencing
a godly sorrow over a sin? Did it lead to
repentance?

5. On the other hand, have you ever experienced
the misery that comes with a private struggle
with sin and a lack of repentance? How did you
finally overcome the sin? (If you did not, are you
open to confessing the sin to a trusted friend
who can steer you back to God's path?)

Chapter 10

Falling Forward

Greatness is not in where we stand, but in what direction we are moving. We must sail sometimes with the wind and sometimes against it—but sail we must and not drift, nor lie at anchor.

—OLIVER WENDELL HOLMES

The first vivid memory I have of sensing God's undeniable presence occurred while singing a worship chorus at a Young Life meeting during my freshman year of high school. Mind you, I only went to Young Life because that's where you could find the cute boys—and particularly, the cute, older boys who could drive. All that to say, I was caught a bit off guard when my heart skipped a beat at the first meeting, not over a cute boy but, rather, while singing a Jesus song. If you are a child of the seventies and eighties, you might remember the familiar song, "Pass It On": "It only takes a spark to get a fire going."[1]

Strangely, I probably learned more about God while singing that one simple song than the sum total of all the bits and pieces of knowledge about Him that I had accumulated in my fifteen years of living in my Bible Belt community.

When I sang "Pass It On," it felt like Jesus had stepped off the front cover of the children's Bible my grandparents had given me at the age of ten and become more than the animated, hippie-looking wanderer who meandered through a green meadow with a cluster of children flanking His sides. When I looked at that picture, I had always assumed the kids were the church kids. Something about singing "Pass It On" made me feel like I was one of those kids—one of the ones on the inside, not on the outside looking in.

My Jesus moments were brief during those years, and they were eventually overshadowed by seemingly more important matters like landing a date to the homecoming dance or making the cheer squad. Holding on to your spot in the popular group was a full-time job and, let's face it, Jesus wasn't always welcome in that group. Except on Young Life meeting nights, where we were given a free pass to love Jesus and not be branded *uncool* in the process. When the meeting was over, most of us left Him behind and rushed back to our full-time professions of being cool. At the time, I didn't realize He was pursuing me in those meetings.

Fast-forward to college. Young Life meetings were in

my rearview mirror, replaced by weekend parties with beer-soaked dance floors, no chaperones, and no curfews. By the time I entered my junior year of college, the partying was beginning to take a toll on me. My drugs of choice (frat parties, alcohol, boyfriends, and so on) were no longer delivering the buzz they once had. On one particular night in my spring semester, I retrieved my children's Bible from the back of my dresser drawer, and in desperation opened it up and began to read. I have no idea what I read, but I do recall asking for help from this God I wasn't sure even existed. I didn't even know what kind of help I was looking for. I just knew I couldn't keep going on the path I was on. His answer to my cry for help came just weeks later—and in the strangest of ways. He showed up, not in church and not as a result of my seeking Him out. He made Himself known during a wild week of spring break partying on a Texas beach.

I was in the parking lot of my rented condo for the week, and my friends and I were icing up a stash of cheap beer for yet another day on the beach when a guy who looked like a fellow college student interrupted us. Strangely, he made a beeline for me, as if I were the only person standing in the parking lot at the time. With all the confidence in the world he looked me straight in the eye and asked, "Would you like to know more about God's love?" He extended his hand in an attempt to hand me what appeared to be a religious tract. I quickly held up my hand in a posture of defense and quipped, "No thanks, but . . . would you like a beer?"

My friends all laughed as he turned and walked away. No doubt he was mumbling a prayer for my hardened heart. My friends marveled at how he had zeroed in on me, joking that it must have been because I had the longest sin list among our bunch. A couple of hours later, while lying on my beach towel with the sound of the waves drowning out the spring break revelry, I thought about that guy. And I thought about his bold question: "Would you like to know more about God's love?" Just weeks ago my answer would have been yes, but I had quickly resumed the only normal life I knew.

Later that night my friends and I were back on the beach to watch the sunset and for another night of partying. The beach was filled with clusters of college kids, most of whom were drinking, throwing a Frisbee, or heckling passersby. And then I heard it. Somewhere off in the distance, I heard music. Jesus music. One of my friends joked that it was probably the same Christian group our friend with the religious tracts had belonged to. We laughed at the thought that the Jesus people had traveled all this way to try to save our lost souls. Another song began to play in the background, and I strained my ears to hear. Something about it sounded so familiar: "It only takes a spark."

Seriously? I thought. Are you kidding me?

I tuned out my friends in an attempt to confirm that it was, in fact, the song I had so loved from the Young Life meetings in high school. Something within my heart began to stir. I felt the strangest desire to walk down the beach and join those

Jesus people; however, I resisted the urge. Fortunately, He didn't give up on me. Several months later a friend invited me to attend a weekend retreat for college students. At that event in 1985, I turned my life over to Christ. I was apprehended by His love after His relentless pursuit.

Remembering

It's important to take the time to remember our roots—the before-and-after stories of our individual journeys to the cross. If you are a believer, you have one. But it's equally as important to remember the bits and pieces of the gospel that intersected your life before you met Christ, those telltale signs of God's pursuit of you along the way. Even if you were young when you came to Christ, chances are you remember defining moments when you felt His undeniable presence in your life. Do you make it a discipline to think back on those moments?

The Bible emphasizes the importance of remembering our before-and-after stories. God told the Israelites to look back and remember. Prior to their exodus from Egypt, they had been held in brutal captivity for over six hundred years, working as slaves under a yoke of oppression. When God stepped in and miraculously delivered them (hello, ten plagues), they didn't call a town meeting when God parted the Red Sea. They didn't question Moses about the proposed meal plan on the Promised Land Tour. They jumped at the chance to be free, even if it meant digging live beetles out of the ground and washing them down with mucky creek water. That wouldn't be necessary, fortunately, because God rained manna down from heaven and brought water from a rock to sustain them during the journey to the Promised Land.

Their newfound taste of freedom didn't last long. Within days of leaving Egypt, they were craving their old way of life—a life of slavery, mind you. "Oh that we had meat to eat! We remember the fish we ate in Egypt that cost nothing, the cucumbers, the melons, the leeks, the onions, and the garlic. But now our strength is dried up, and there is nothing at all but this manna to look at" (Num. 11:4–6).

Bless their hearts. The Israelites demonstrated a textbook example of selective memory. They suffered from a severe case of retrograde amnesia, forgetting the *before* story. As a reminder, here's a brief description of their lives in captivity prior to God's deliverance: "So they ruthlessly made the people of Israel work as slaves and made their lives bitter with hard service, in mortar and brick, and in all kinds of work in the field. In all their work they ruthlessly made them work as slaves" (Ex. 1:13–14). And who could forget: "Then Pharaoh commanded all his people, 'Every son that is born to the Hebrews you shall cast into the Nile, but you shall let every daughter live'" (Ex. 1:22).

Well, goodness gracious. "The cucumbers! The melons! And garlic! I mean, who can eat manna without garlic?! Let's go back to Egypt and eat some real food! Never mind the part about working as slave labor round the clock, the brutal beatings, and throwing our newborn sons into the

Nile. It's a small price to pay for good food, no?" Selective memory at its best. Look, I feel their pain of a diet without proper seasonings. I salt everything before I taste it, including pepperoni pizza. But I think I'd be willing to forego the salt and the pizza and live off of a steady diet of manna if I didn't have to worry about my sons being tossed into the Nile. No amount of counseling will help you recover from that one.

In reality, the manna was hardly worthy of complaint. Exodus 16:31 says that "the taste of it was like wafers made with honey." We're talking graham crackers, people. I'll take that any day over a melon or cucumber. Granted, eating the same thing every day could get a bit tiresome and cause most of us to get a little grouchy, but had they already forgotten what they *used to* grumble about? "The people of Israel groaned because of their slavery and cried out for help. Their cry for rescue from slavery came up to God. And God heard their groaning, and God remembered his covenant with Abraham, with Isaac, and with Jacob" (Ex. 2:23–24).

It's easy to read about the Israelites' memory loss and walk away thinking, *What a bunch of idiots. If I were in their shoes, I'd never complain.* In truth, you and I are no different when it comes to our own stories of deliverance and the whining we often do. We come to a place where we cry out to God for His grace and mercy. God delivers. We are forever grateful—in the moment. We ride on the coattails of grace in the days that follow. But then life happens. The monotonies of daily living begin to take their toll. Piles of laundry. A complaining spouse. An unbearable in-law. An ungrateful child. Challenges at church. Another school project. Life gets hard and busy. Very busy. Before long, the dark and painful days that led us to Christ begin to fade in our memory. When we don't take time to reflect back, the details begin to blur, and over time we're left with a more sanitized, polished, less sinful version of our pre-Christian selves or, perhaps, a glossed-over CliffsNotes version. We minimize the brutalizing captivity of sin and sugarcoat the events that led us to fall on our knees at the foot of the cross. And some of us, just like those Israelites, may have a tendency to look back with longing for a taste of our old lives. Times when we could simply numb ourselves with alcohol, shopping, or activities. Times when going through the motions was easier than living with heart and courage. Times when walking away from our husband and children was an option. Times when it felt good to be irresponsible and rebellious.

That longing for Egypt is exactly why God commands us to practice the discipline of "remembering." When we don't take the time to remember, it's only a matter of time before we forget. We will forget the pain of slavery. Forget our first desperate taste of freedom. Forget the power of the gospel. Forget how we wanted to share the gospel with everyone we met. And when we forget, it's only a matter of time before our faith becomes routine or, even worse, we get stuck in the quicksand of mediocrity. We cannot move on, and we cannot move forward unless we look back at the times when Mercy met us in our mess and changed our futures.

Unstuck in a Rut

If ever there was a playbook for moving on in our journey of faith, the apostle Paul offered the solution in Philippians 3:12–14:

> Not that I have already obtained this or am already perfect, but I press on to make it my own, because Christ Jesus has made me his own. Brothers, I do not consider that I have made it my own. But one thing I do: forgetting what lies behind and straining forward to what lies ahead, I press on toward the goal for the prize of the upward call of God in Christ Jesus.

Paul spoke two powerful words to those stuck in a rut of mediocrity: *press on.* "Not that I have already obtained this or am already perfect . . ." Paul knew when he left the starting blocks he would not run a perfect race. One Bible commentary notes,

> This very sense of imperfection urges the Christian to sustained effort. He is never satisfied with himself, therefore he always presses onwards. He does not dwell with complacency on his attainments, but forgets the progress which he has made; in view of the far greater height which remains to scale, he throws himself into the work with ever-increasing energy. Therefore he presses toward the mark.[2]

What is "the mark" for those of us who run the Christian race? Our Savior who waits at the finish. The race has already been won. God is not standing at the finish line with stop-watch in hand, shaking His head back and forth in disapproval as we limp toward Him. That's not what Mercy looks like. Running a perfect race was never the goal. Choosing to fol-low Him despite the allure of sin and the trials of this life is the goal we strive for every day. Jesus, in all of His glory and perfection, stands waiting for us at the end of the journey.

Until we cross over the finish line, we will struggle. We will face the temptation to stop dead in our tracks and walk off the path. Instead, we choose to strain forward to what lies ahead. The Greek word for *straining* is *ĕpĕktĕinŏmai*, which means "to stretch (oneself) forward; reach forth."[3] It's awfully hard to stretch forward when you've assumed the posture of a down-and-out face-plant on the track or relegated yourself to sitting on the sidelines. When Paul wrote to the Philippians, he'd been running the Christian race for about thirty years, so he had experienced plenty of interruptions in the race. He wasn't surprised when he encountered them. He expected them. He knew that "two steps forward and one step back" is still progress. He didn't allow the roadblocks along the course to stall his journey. He pressed on, despite the cost.

I began this book by talking about the importance of let-ting ourselves off the hook when it comes to being perfect. True freedom comes when we can finally give ourselves per-mission to not be "great, thank you"—but to be strugglers in the race. Again, we don't want to stay where we are, but rather we rely on the only One who can help us move on in the journey. "But one thing I do: forgetting what lies behind and straining forward to what lies ahead, I press on . . ." What is holding you up in this race?

Are you are bogged down by circumstances that are outside of your control? Mercy is waiting to comfort you. With Mercy's help you can move on.

Are you delayed in the race because of your own sin? Mercy is waiting to rescue you. With Mercy's help you can move on.

Have you been pretending so long that you still show up for the race (that is, go to church) but your heart left a long time ago? Mercy is waiting to jump-start your faith. With Mercy's help you can remember why you started running this race in the first place, and it can give you the desire to keep moving.

Moving on is only possible when our hearts are yielded to Christ and reliant upon His mercy and perfection. At the end of the Philippians 3 challenge, Paul encouraged believers, "Let those of us who are mature think this way, and if in anything you think otherwise, God will reveal that also to you. Only let us hold true to what we have attained" (vv. 15–16). One commentary notes,

> The apostle called his readers to share with him the pursuit of Christlikeness. What he wanted for himself he also wanted for them. "All of us who are mature should take such a view of things (v. 15)". What view of things? The one [view] he had expressed regarding persistently pressing on toward the goal. One mark of spiritual maturity is a desire to *go on with Christ* [emphasis mine]. Paul's appeal here was to maturing believers who shared his ambitions.[4]

I love that: "Go on with Christ." The commentary goes on to say, "The greatest need among God's people is to live up to what they already have in Christ. Most live far below their exalted position in Christ. Paul's plea to the Philippians was that they live up to what they had already attained, namely a righteous position in Christ."[5]

Paul refused to let his imperfections, his stumbling steps, and the hurdles get the best of him because he knew the race had already been won. Thanks to Jesus' victory on the cross, Paul was declared a winner before he ever finished the race. The prize was his to claim at the finish—to see His Savior face-to-face. The same promise is true for believers today. We, too, have been declared winners. Why then do we often run as if the race is still ours to win or lose? Why do we think that it's ultimately about us? Why do we mark our lives by our mistakes rather than by the growth God births in us? No wonder we get stuck along the way!

Falling Down Versus Falling Forward

It was a typical sweltering Austin afternoon as my husband and I found a spot to sit in the crowded metal bleachers at the regional track meet. Our son was warming up on the field for the 4x100 relay. There were several more races to go before he and his teammates would line up in the starting blocks. My husband and I were talking to another couple when the gun sounded in the distance and our voices were muffled by the cheering crowd. Finally giving up on finishing our conversation, we focused our eyes on the track to watch the 110m hurdles race in progress. And that's when I saw him. A young runner approached the first set of hurdles, but his back foot tipped the hurdle and he tumbled to the ground. The crowd instantly reacted to his fall by uttering a guttural, universal groan.

I watched as the young man got back up and headed for the next hurdle. Mind you, most of the other young men were approaching the finish line at this point, so his fate was already sealed. He would finish in last place regardless of whether or not he completed the race. I could hardly believe my eyes as I watched him miss the next hurdle, stumbling and falling forward until he again tumbled to the ground. My heart ached for this boy as the crowd let out another collective groan. I heard a spectator yell, "It's okay, son. You don't have to finish the race." Clearly, walking off the track without finishing was not an option for this guy. He struggled to his feet yet again and headed for the next hurdle. I'm pretty sure everyone in the stands was holding their breath at this point. I want so badly to tell you that he cleared that next hurdle, and the next, and the next, but that didn't happen.

He didn't clear a single hurdle in the race. Not one.

Anyone else would have walked off the track and called it a day, but not this boy. He was dead set and determined to cross the finish line at any cost. Ribbon or not, this young man was a winner as far as I was concerned. I had to wonder, *What makes this boy different?* What drove him to finish when so many others would have given up? The answer is simple:

some people fall *down* and others fall *forward*. Those who simply fall down make getting back up their primary goal. Their next step is yet to be determined. Finish or not finish? Play it safe and walk off the track—or forge ahead and risk another stumble? Those who fall forward, however, look at the race differently. Their primary focus is crossing the finish line. Getting back up is a given. Future stumbles are factored into the equation. They've accepted the truth that hurdles are an inevitable part of this race called life and that they will face struggles and heartache along the way. They don't look around and compare themselves or their progress in the race to the other runners. They don't look ahead to the faster ones. They don't try to measure up to the polished ones. They don't even envy the ones who appear to clear the hurdles with ease. Those who fall forward keep their line of vision on the finish line, not on the other runners ahead or behind them. The writer of Hebrews echoed this idea when he wrote,

> Therefore, since we are surrounded by so great a cloud of witnesses, let us also lay aside every weight, and sin which clings so closely, and let us run with endurance the race that is set before us, looking to Jesus, the founder and perfecter of our faith, who for the joy that was set before him endured the cross, despising the shame, and is seated at the right hand of the throne of God. (12:1–2)

Interestingly, the Greek word for *race* is *agon*, which is the root for the word *agony* used in Luke 22:44: "And being in an agony he prayed more earnestly; and his sweat became like great drops of blood falling down to the ground."[6] *Agon* is also the root for the word *fought* in 2 Timothy 4:7, where Paul boldly declared as he approached the finish line: "I have fought a good fight, I have finished my course, I have kept the faith" (kjv).[7]

My course. Not the course I necessarily scripted for myself, but *my course* nonetheless. Not the course some of my Christian sisters are running that looks so smooth and straight, but my course. Not the course proposed in the latest how-to-love-Jesus-better book or blog, but my course. Not the course of my parents, my husband, or my children, but my course. God only asks that I run my *personal* race. God designed this course for me. It's not like anyone else's, nor is it to be compared to anyone else's. He wants me to own my course because my course is part of His bigger story—a story that points to His goodness, grace, and mercy.

The race is messy. You've probably figured that out by now, many of you the hard way. You will face building-high hurdles and Grand Canyon–wide potholes on the course, and you'll veer off the path at times. You'll find yourself stuck in a few muddy ruts on the course, some that may leave you dirt-caked and downtrodden for years. And some days you will think you can't take another step and you will want to give up the race altogether.

It's an arduous marathon, but you won't ever run alone. Mercy will never leave your side.

Again and again He whispers, *My grace is sufficient for you.*

You don't always hear Him.

My power is made perfect in weakness.

You don't always look up to see Him.

You can do this. We can do this together.

You don't always listen.

Take My hand. Trust Me.

You don't always trust Him.

Set your sight on the finish line, where your prize awaits.

It's time to move on.

COMING CLEAN

1. Can you recall moments when you felt God's undeniable presence in your life? Describe those moments.

2. Is there an area of your spiritual life that is in need of improvement? If so, what steps do you plan to take to reach that goal?

3. In the previous chapters we discussed common ruts that can result in a mediocre faith. Which of the ruts have you found yourself in? Which one is the biggest struggle for you right now?

4. When you read Philippians 3:12–14, what verses do you find most encouraging? Why?

5. Share an example of a time when you "pressed on" in the race.

6. Would you say you are more likely to fall down or fall forward when encountering various hurdles in the race? Why?

7. What are some practical steps God may be nudging you to take in an effort to move on in your race of faith?

Acknowledgments

I am blessed with a long list of people who have played a role through the years in my move-on journey. Some have offered a shoulder to cry on or a much-needed listening ear. Others have provided a timely word or a gentle nudge to get me back on track. Yet others have been a safe place for me to be honest about my struggles and weaknesses. It would be impossible to name them all, but here are a few who top the list.

My husband, Keith: When I think back on the twenty-seven years we've been together, I don't recognize the couple who stood at the altar and said, "I do" in 1987. And I'm not just talking about how we've aged! As a couple, we have done a whole lot of *moving on*, and our marriage has been richer for it. There is no greater joy than doing life with your very best friend. I continue to be in awe of your never-wavering faith and godliness. I am a blessed, blessed girl.

To my grown children, Ryan and Casey, Paige and Matt, and Hayden: What a joy it is to be *friends* with your children!

I am so thankful we don't play the pretender game in this family and have granted each other permission to be fellow strugglers in this journey of faith. May we always put God's grace in the spotlight where it belongs.

My dearest friends: Barbara, Damon, Carolyn, and Donnie. What would Keith and I do without you guys? We have shared joys, heartaches, parenting frustrations, and ministry challenges. We have solved the problems of the world on the front porch of the lake house and laughed until our sides ached. Over the years we have shared more memories than I can begin to count. Thank you for always being *safe friends*.

My brother, Scott, and my aunt, Cynthia: Thank you for walking with me through a very painful and stormy chapter. The sun is breaking through the clouds, and sunny days are ahead. It's time to move on.

The women who have confided with me through the years about their own personal messes: Your willingness to come clean taught me that moving on isn't possible unless we are first willing to acknowledge the mess. Your courage to remove your masks gave me courage to remove my own.

I also want to recognize Debbie Wickwire, who has been a constant cheerleader to me throughout this publishing process. Thank you, friend, for believing in this message.

Last of all, I have acknowledged my literary agent, Lee Hough, in every book I've written since we began working together in 2004. Unfortunately, Lee lost his battle to brain cancer before this book went to print. I was fortunate, though, to see him several weeks before he was promoted to heaven and handed him this acknowledgement in advance:

Lee, you were a huge champion of the message of this book and cheered me on through countless rewrites of the proposal. This book would not have happened had you not believed in me and taken a chance on a newbie author back in 2004, with only one book under her belt. I truly felt like I'd won the lottery when you agreed to represent me on that day nearly ten years ago. Over the years, when asked who was my agent, I would proudly reply, "Lee Hough," and beam from ear to ear. The mere mention of your name was always met with high praises for your abilities as an agent and, most important, your character and integrity as a man of God. I'm a blessed girl to have been one of "Lee Hough's authors" and even more blessed to call you a friend.

And to Lee's sweet wife, Paula: As you attempt to move on without your best friend by your side, may you feel Mercy's clear, undeniable presence in the days ahead.

Notes

Chapter 1: Cleanup on Aisle One!

1. Stasi Eldredge, *Becoming Myself: Embracing God's Dream of You* (Colorado Springs: David C. Cook, 2013), 20–21.
2. Brennan Manning, *The Ragamuffin Gospel: Good News for the Bedraggled, Beat-Up, and Burnt Out* (New York: Random House, 2008), 220.
3. "Stained Glass Masquerade," written by Mark Hall and Nichole Nordeman, performed by Casting Crowns, *Lifesong*, Reunion Records, 2005, compact disc.
4. William Shakespeare, *Hamlet*, Act 1, scene 3, line 79.
5. Margery Williams, *The Velveteen Rabbit* (New York: George H. Doran, 1922), 29.
6. James Strong, *A Concise Dictionary of the Words in the Greek Testament and the Hebrew Bible* (Bellingham, WA: Logos Research Systems, Inc., 2009), s. v. "charis."

Chapter 2: Sanitized for Your Protection

1. "Amazing Grace," lyrics by John Newton (1725–1807).
2. James Strong, *A Concise Dictionary of the Words in the Greek Testament and the Hebrew Bible* (Bellingham, WA: Logos Research Systems, Inc., 2009), s. v. "katĕrgazŏmai."

3. Strong, *A Concise Dictionary*, s. v. "chara."
4. Matt Redman and Beth Redman, "Blessed Be Your Name," performed by Matt Redman, *Where Angels Fear to Tread*, Survivor Records, 2002, compact disc.
5. Charles Spurgeon, quoted in W. R. Funk, "The Mercies of the Lord," editorial, *The Religious Telescope* (Dayton, Ohio), January 20, 1904.
6. Twitter post, August 23, 2013, 07:41:44 GMT, https://twitter.com /CSLewisDaily.

Chapter 3: Us and Them

1. Soulforce, www.soulforce.com.

Chapter 4: Unclaimed Baggage

1. Beth Moore, *James: Mercy Triumphs* (Nashville: LifeWay Christian Resources, 2011), 181.
2. James Strong, *A Concise Dictionary of the Words in the Greek Testament and the Hebrew Bible* (Bellingham, WA: Logos Research Systems, Inc., 2009), s. v. "ĕpilanthanŏmai."

Chapter 5: Buried Alive

1. Dictionary.com, s. v. "shame," accessed December 3, 2013, http:// dictionary.reference.com/browse/shame?s=t.
2. Mark Twain, "Pudd'nhead Wilson's New Calendar," in *Following the Equator*.
3. Lewis B. Smedes, *Shame and Grace* (HarperSan Francisco, 1993), ix.
4. John Bradshaw, *Healing the Shame That Binds You*, rev. ed. (New York: HCI, 2005), 5, 29–30.
5. Bible Hub, s. v. "thanatos," accessed December 4, 2013, http:// biblehub.com/greek/2288.htm.
6. "Dr. Brené Brown: 'Shame Is Lethal,'" Oprah.com, March 24, 2013, http://www.oprah.com/own-super-soul-sunday /Dr-Brene-Brown-Shame-Is-Lethal-Video.
7. Dictionary.com, s. v. "shame," accessed December 3, 2013, http:// dictionary.reference.com/browse/shame?s=t.

8. Michael Cheshire, "Going to Hell with Ted Haggard," ChristianityToday.com, December 3, 2012, http://www. christianitytoday.com/le/2012 /december-online-only/going-to-hell-with-ted-haggard.html.

9. James Strong, *A Concise Dictionary of the Words in the Greek Testament and the Hebrew Bible* (Bellingham, WA: Logos Research Systems, Inc., 2009), s. v. "plērŏphŏria."

10. Blue Letter Bible, s. v. "kataginōskō," accessed December 3, 2013, http://www.blueletterbible.org/lang/lexicon/lexicon .cfm?Strongs=G2607&t=KJV.

11. "Texas Judge Orders Convicted Drunk Driver to Public Humiliation," FoxNews.com, April 21, 2012, http://www .foxnews.com/us/2012/04/21/texas-judge-orders-convicted-drunk -driver-to-public-humiliation/#ixzz2W0mldFOZ.

12. Brian Palmer, "Can We Bring Back the Stockades? The Constitutionality of Public Shaming," Slate.com, November 15, 2012, http://www.slate.com/articles/news_and_politics /explainer/2012/11/public_shaming_sentences_can_judges_subject _criminals_to_humiliation.html.

13. Ibid.

14. IVP New Testament Commentaries, "Jesus Forgives a Woman Taken in Adultery," accessed December 3, 2013, http://www .biblegateway.com/resources/commentaries/IVP-NT/John /Jesus-Forgives-Woman-Taken.

Chapter 6: Law and Disorder

1. Gary Cartwright, "The Terror of Tarrytown: How an Animal Rights Zealot Ruined My Favorite Shopping Center," *Texas Monthly*, September 2007, http://www.texasmonthly.com/story /terror-tarrytown.

2. Dictionary.com, s. v. "legalism," accessed October 1, 2013, http:// dictionary.reference.com/browse/legalism?s=t&ld=1170.

3. Hon. Benjamin Harrison, "Reverence for the Bible," *The Ladies' Home Journal*, April 1896, 14.

4. Blue Letter Bible, s. v. "hupŏkritēs," accessed October 1, 2013, http://www.blueletterbible.org/lang/lexicon/lexicon .cfm?strongs=G5273&t=NIV.

5. This quote has been widely attributed to German philosopher and poet Johann Wolfgang von Goethe (1749–1832).

Chapter 7: Get More "Likes"!

1. James Strong, *A Concise Dictionary of the Words in the Greek Testament and the Hebrew Bible* (Bellingham, WA: Logos Research Systems, Inc., 2009), s. v. "môqêsh."
2. Strong, *A Concise Dictionary*, s. v. "ĕti."

Chapter 8: Buzz-Hopping

1. Timothy Keller, *Counterfeit Gods: The Empty Promises of Money, Sex, and Power, and the Only Hope That Matters* (New York: Dutton Publishing, 2009), 17.
2. C. S. Lewis, *The Problem of Pain* (San Francisco: HarperCollins, 1996), 106–7.
3. John Owen, *The Mortification of Sin*, abridged ed. (Carlisle, PA: Banner of Truth, 2004), 748.
4. Brennan Manning, *The Ragamuffin Gospel: Good News for the Bedraggled, Beat-Up, and Burnt Out* (New York: Random House, 2008), 85.
5. Renee Swope, *A Confident Heart: How to Stop Doubting Yourself and Live in the Security of God's Promises* (Ada, MI: Revell, 2011), 55.

Chapter 9: Prone to Wander

1. Donald Miller, Twitter post, July 15, 2013, 11:47 a.m., https://twitter.com/donaldmiller/status/353193327711096833.
2. D. L. Moody, "New Things," *The Christian Week: A Weekly Record of Evangelical Thought and Work*, June 29, 1881, 611.
3. Brennan Manning, *Abba's Child: The Cry of the Heart for Intimate Belonging* (Colorado Springs: NavPress, 2009), 44.
4. Kevin Dolak, "Homeless Nephew of Millionaire Heiress Died Standing to Inherit $19 Million," abcnews.com, December 31, 2012, http://abcnews.go.com/US/homeless-nephew-millionaire-heiress-died-standing-inherit-19/story?id=18102186.

5. Steve McVey, *52 Lies Heard in Church Every Sunday: And Why the Truth Is So Much Better* (Eugene, OR: Harvest House, 2011), 13.

6. Charles Spurgeon, quoted in Warren Wiersbe, *The Wycliffe Handbook of Preaching and Preachers* (Chicago, IL: Moody Press, 1984), 235.

7. Brother Lawrence, *The Brother Lawrence Collection* (Radford, VA: Wilder Publications, 2008), 24.

8. Jerry Bridges, *The Discipline of Grace: God's Role and Our Role in the Pursuit of Holiness* (Colorado Springs: NavPress, 2006), 27.

9. "Come Thou Fount of Every Blessing," lyrics by Robert Robinson, (1735–1790).

10. Kenneth W. Osbeck, *101 Hymn Stories* (Grand Rapids, MI: Kregel Publications, 1982), 52.

11. C. S. Lewis, *Mere Christianity* (San Francisco: Harper San Francisco, 2009), 28–29.

Chapter 10: Falling Forward

1. "Pass It On," written by Kurt Kaiser, Lexicon Music, 1969.

2. H. D. M. Spence–Jones and Joseph Excell, *The Pulpit Commentary: Philippians* (Bellingham, WA: Logos Research Systems, Inc., 2004), 119.

3. James Strong, *A Concise Dictionary of the Words in the Greek Testament and the Hebrew Bible* (Bellingham, WA: Logos Research Systems, Inc., 2009), s. v. "ĕpĕktĕinŏmai."

4. John F. Walvoord and Roy B. Zuck, eds., *The Bible Knowledge Commentary: An Exposition of the Scriptures by Dallas Seminary Faculty* (Wheaton, IL: Victor Books, 1983), s. v. "Philippians 3:15–16."

5. Ibid.

6. Strong, *A Concise Dictionary*, s. v. "agon."

7. Ibid.

About the Author

Vicki Courtney is a national speaker to women of all ages and the best-selling author of many books and Bible studies including *5 Conversations You Must Have with Your Daughter* and *Ever After*.

But that was not the original road she was traveling—as a self-proclaimed agnostic and feminist in her twenties, Vicki got talked into signing up for a weekend retreat for college students. The event, sponsored by a local Baptist church, was not on her list of weekend hangouts, but she went and was moved by the clear presentation of the gospel. After eleven choruses of "I Have Decided to Follow Jesus," her icy heart melted, and she said yes to God.

Not a day goes by that she is not floored by the platform God has graciously given her. Her prayer is that everything she does will point to His goodness and mercy. Vicki and her husband live in Austin, Texas, near their three children, son-in-love, daughter-in-love, and grandson.

Also Available from Vicki Courtney

In this six-session video-based curriculum, author and speaker Vicki Courtney discusses how most people live their entire lives attempting to clean up messes on their own or hide their issues under a multitude of modern-day fig leaves. She encourages those who are weary of hiding and pretending to find the courage to come clean about the mess they are—to lay their hearts and souls bare before the Lord and say, "I'm not okay, and I need your help." The study guide includes individual and group activities, between-session personal studies, and additional material that will enhance your experience of the video sessions.

W PUBLISHING GROUP

AN IMPRINT OF THOMAS NELSON

Available wherever books and Bibles are sold